D0056752

Praise for *Power Questions*

"We all strive to create genuine human connection with clients, friends, and family. *Power Questions* is a tremendous, practical guide to constructing and using the powerful questions that help you do this. Read it now, take it in deeply, put it into practice, and it will transform your conversations and perhaps your life."

—**Steve Thomas,**
President of Global Sales, Experian

"What did FDR, Socrates, Shakespeare, and Jesus have in common? According to Sobel and Panas, they all knew how to ask 'power questions.' Read this book and you will too!"

—**Marshall Goldsmith,**
Author of the *New York Times* best-sellers *MOJO* and *What Got
You Here Won't Get You There

"*Power Questions* is a fresh, incisive, and compelling guide to achieving success in our personal and professional relationships and activities. The book methodically maps out the route to employ carefully chosen questions that will elicit the most helpful responses and achieve the most desirable outcomes. It's a must-read!"

—**The Honorable Joseph P. Riley,**
Mayor, Charleston, South Carolina

"Congratulations. The name says it all. It is a powerful book. *Power Questions* is a must-read for anyone who cares about customers, employees, and investors. My recommendation to everyone is to pick up a copy now and read it."

—**Robert L. Dilenschneider,**
Chief Executive Officer and Chairman,
The Dilenschneider Group, Inc.

"*Power Questions* provides the vital building blocks to successfully understanding the needs of your customers and clients, your spouse or child. The book describes the necessary skills needed to ask the right questions in the right way. A masterpiece. The book is compelling."

—Robert Milligan,
Past Chairman, United States Chamber of Commerce
and Founder and Chair, Nature's Variety

"Asking clients good questions leads to great conversations, and the result is trusted client relationships. *Power Questions* is a terrific read full of captivating examples. It will help readers develop deeper, more valuable relationships in both their professional and social lives."

—James Bardrick,
Managing Director and Banking
Co-Head for Europe, Middle East,
and Africa, Citigroup

"*Power Questions* is an amazing book about having real power in your life—power to solve problems while developing deep relationships with others and also a better understanding of yourself."

—Cal Turner,
Former Chief Executive Officer
and Chairman of the Board,
Dollar General

"*Why should I care what you think until I know that you care?* I learned these words of wisdom from a very successful man. Now, Panas and Sobel answer the question, "How do I show that I care?" It is by asking thoughtful, powerful questions and listening carefully to the answers. You'll learn, you'll care, you'll build trust and understanding. *Power Questions* is outstanding."

—B. Joseph White,
President Emeritus,
James F. Towey Professor of
Business and Leadership,
University of Illinois and author
of best-selling *The Nature of Leadership*

"I found *Power Questions* so relevant I am making it required reading for all of my employees. Andrew and Jerry remind us of the vital importance of listening intensely. The book gives us the tools to get invaluable and rewarding information. This is a resource for life."

—Aristotle Halikias,
Chief Executive Officer and
Chairman of the Board,
Republic Bank

"While reading *Power Questions*, I made lists of hundreds of questions I can use. I've always struggled to ask good, open-ended, and probing questions that allow me to learn so much about another person. This book has helped me jump that hurdle. It is tremendously thought-provoking and at the same time, extremely entertaining. If you've read every other book Andrew Sobel and Jerry Panas have written, you may think they couldn't top themselves—but they do in *Power Questions*."

—Michelle Easton,
President, Clare Boothe
Luce Policy Institute

"*Power Questions* is for everyone—salespeople, supervisors, development officers, and even parents. Jerry Panas and Andrew Sobel inform us how to ask the very best questions in a manner most likely to elicit an insightful answer. The authors provide hundreds of questions you wish you had asked. *Power Questions* will ensure your meetings and conversations are more productive than ever before. It should be required reading—and it will be in my organization."

—Ron Robinson,
Author, *Funding Fathers*

"Ask yourself: Can I afford not to read *Power Questions*? Andrew and Jerry's book is refreshingly different, packed full of anecdotes and advice that will give you the questions you need to engage, enquire, and elicit. Easy to read, I found plenty of new ideas to help me deepen my client relationships."

—Diana Brightmore-Armour,
CEO, Corporate Banking,
Lloyds Banking Group

"Your relationships will never be the same. Organized and written in a highly accessible 'story-telling' style, *Power Questions* is as entertaining as it is deep, and its lessons and value are as relevant and powerful for any Fortune 500 CEO as they are for a teacher, parent, or my 14-year-old son. Andrew Sobel and Jerry Panas have distilled the art of communicating down to the core skill of crafting and posing 'the right' questions at 'the right' times—questions that open doors and engender the engagement necessary to build meaningful relationships and true connectivity."

—Adam L. Reeder,
Managing Director and Global
Head of Building Products
and Basic Materials,
Credit Suisse First Boston

POWER
QUESTIONS

Build Relationships,
Win New Business,
and Influence Others

ANDREW   JEROLD
SOBEL   **PANAS**

WILEY

John Wiley & Sons, Inc.

Copyright © 2012 by Andrew Sobel and Jerold Panas. All rights reserved.

Published by John Wiley & Sons, Inc., Hoboken, New Jersey.
Published simultaneously in Canada.

No part of this publication may be reproduced, stored in a retrieval system, or transmitted in any form or by any means, electronic, mechanical, photocopying, recording, scanning, or otherwise, except as permitted under Section 107 or 108 of the 1976 United States Copyright Act, without either the prior written permission of the Publisher, or authorization through payment of the appropriate per-copy fee to the Copyright Clearance Center, Inc., 222 Rosewood Drive, Danvers, MA 01923, (978) 750-8400, fax (978) 646-8600, or on the web at www.copyright.com. Requests to the Publisher for permission should be addressed to the Permissions Department, John Wiley & Sons, Inc., 111 River Street, Hoboken, NJ 07030, (201) 748-6011, fax (201) 748-6008, or online at http://www.wiley.com/go/permissions.

Limit of Liability/Disclaimer of Warranty: While the publisher and author have used their best efforts in preparing this book, they make no representations or warranties with respect to the accuracy or completeness of the contents of this book and specifically disclaim any implied warranties of merchantability or fitness for a particular purpose. No warranty may be created or extended by sales representatives or written sales materials. The advice and strategies contained herein may not be suitable for your situation. You should consult with a professional where appropriate. Neither the publisher nor author shall be liable for any loss of profit or any other commercial damages, including but not limited to special, incidental, consequential, or other damages.

For general information on our other products and services or for technical support, please contact our Customer Care Department within the United States at (800) 762-2974, outside the United States at (317) 572-3993 or fax (317) 572-4002.

Wiley publishes in a variety of print and electronic formats and by print-on-demand. Some material included with standard print versions of this book may not be included in e-books or in print-on-demand. If this book refers to media such as a CD or DVD that is not included in the version you purchased, you may download this material at http://booksupport.wiley.com. For more information about Wiley products, visit www.wiley.com.

ISBN 978-1-118-11963-1 (cloth); ISBN 978-1-118-21847-1 (ebk); ISBN 978-1-118-21848-8 (ebk); ISBN 978-1-118-21849-5 (ebk)

Printed in the United States of America

10 9 8 7 6 5 4 3 2 1

*To all the men and women who wish to build
fresh and exciting relationships, thrive professionally,
and motivate all you come in
contact with—this book is dedicated to you.
If you believe, as we do, that most often
the question is more important than the answer,
you are well on your way to success
at work and in life.*

Contents

The Power
Questions

1 | Good Questions Trump Easy Answers

We're sitting comfortably in a sun-filled office on the fortieth floor of a Chicago skyscraper. We ask the CEO, "What most impresses you when you meet someone who is trying to win your business? What builds trust and credibility with you early on in a relationship?"

This executive runs a $12-billion company. We are interviewing him about his most trusted business relationships. These are the service providers and suppliers his company goes back to again and again, the individuals who are part of his inner circle of trusted advisors.

"I can always tell," he says, "how experienced and insightful a prospective consultant, banker, or lawyer is by the quality of their *questions* and how intently they listen. That's how simple it is."

In a direct but sweeping statement about what builds a relationship, he tells us what hundred of others we've advised and interviewed also affirm: *Good questions are often far more powerful than answers.*

Good questions challenge your thinking. They reframe and redefine the problem. They throw cold water on our most dearly held assumptions, and force us out of our traditional thinking. They motivate us to learn and discover more. They remind us of what is most important in our lives.

In ancient history, transformational figures such as Socrates and Jesus used questions to great effect. Their questions were teaching tools and also a means to change indelibly the people around them. We'll meet both in later chapters and learn their techniques.

But you'll also meet corporate leaders, a minister, a billionaire, an attorney, a medical center CEO, and dozens more. They are all fascinating people (some you may know), for whom a power question becomes a pivotal turning point.

In the twentieth century, towering intellectuals such as Albert Einstein and Peter Drucker loved to ask provocative questions.

One morning a young Einstein watched the sun glittering off a field of flowers. He asked himself, "Could I travel on that beam of light? Could I reach or exceed the speed of light?" Later, he told a friend, "I have no special talents. I am only passionately curious."

Drucker is considered to be one of the most profound thinkers in the field of management. He was famous for his intense questioning sessions with clients.

Rather than offering advice, Drucker would pose simple but penetrating questions such as, "What business are you really in?" And, "What do your customers value most?"

When a journalist once referred to him as a consultant, Drucker objected. He said he was actually an "insultant"—a nod to the tough, direct questions he liked to ask his clients.

Great artists have always understood the role of questions. It is no accident that the most famous dramatic passage in all of literature is built around a single question. "To be, or not to be, that is the question," says Shakespeare's Prince Hamlet as he contemplates life and death.

We use the phrase *power questions* as the title of this book. That's because the questions we select have the power to give new life to your conversations in unexpected and delightful ways. They are powerful tools to get directly to the heart of the matter. They are the keys to opening locked doors.

Each of the next 34 short chapters recounts a conversation or situation that was transformed through one or more power questions. We've used real-life examples in order to illustrate how and when to use the questions. In the final section of this book, called "Not Just for Sunday," we list another 293 power questions. Using these additional questions will help you succeed in a variety of professional and personal situations.

Learning to use the power of questions can dramatically increase your professional and personal effectiveness. This book will help you build and deepen relationships. Sell more of your products, services, and ideas. Motivate others to give more effort than they ever thought possible. And become more effective at influencing clients, colleagues, and friends.

Are you ready to use the transformational power of great questions? Read on.

2 | If You Don't Want to Hit Bottom, Stop Digging the Hole

Even when I think about it today, it still makes me cringe. It was an embarrassing moment of youthful naïveté. I wanted to shine, but I fell flat on my face.

The 1960s pop group Procol Harum said it perfectly when they sang, "My befuddled brain is shining brightly, quite insane."

We're meeting with a major telecommunications company that my consulting firm wants to do business with. I'm a newly promoted partner in the firm. I am eager—oh, so eager—to make my mark by acquiring a major new client.

I'm determined to make this meeting a success. I arrive armed to the teeth. Masses of supporting evidence. We will establish ourselves as not just the best choice but the *only* consultant of choice for this company.

There are three of us and five of them. Several of their group are vice presidents with significant responsibilities. Not at the top, but senior enough. They invite us into a spacious conference room. It's not the boardroom—the table has a black laminated top instead of hardwood. But it's sufficiently elegant. We look around approvingly.

I bring thick binders for them. Hefty decks of PowerPoint slides. Plenty of in-depth documentation.

It turns out that was absolutely the wrong kind of preparation.

I should have studied Woodrow Wilson. He said, "If I am to speak 10 minutes, I need a week for preparation. If 15 minutes, three days. If half an hour, two days. If an hour, I am ready now." I was certainly not prepared for brevity.

Then the first question from the client, the initial salvo. It's a softball pitch. Hard to mess that up.

"Tell us a bit about yourselves."

I want to leave no doubt in their minds that we are uniquely qualified to help them. I tell them about the history of our firm, how it was formed by the merger of two other consulting firms. Having lived through it myself, I thought the story fascinating.

I describe our client base. I walk though some of our most important methodologies. I tell them about our joint-team approach to collaborating with clients. About how well we listen (I am too young to appreciate the irony of that claim).

I cannot bear to spare any of the essential facts. Facts that I know will impress them and make them quick to retain us. On the spot.

I am so focused on our qualifications, however, that I pretty much forget the client on the other side of the table. I don't realize how fast time flies when you're talking.

After nearly 30 minutes, my colleagues and I finally stop our presentation. There is silence.

One of the vice presidents reaches for something in a pile of folders. Is it a copy of their strategic plan they want to share with us? An organization chart to illustrate who else we should speak to at the company?

No. She is grabbing her appointment book. "This has been very helpful, thank you. I really do have to run to another meeting now."

It's too late! We have built little personal rapport—actually none. We have achieved virtually no understanding of their goals, their issues, or their challenges. We lost our chance. Now we're being escorted out.

(Writing this, I hear the refrain from Bob Dylan's song "My Back Pages" echoing in my head: "Ah, but I was so much older then, I'm younger than that now." I'm reminded there are no mistakes in life, only lessons).

Fast forward. It's now a year later. I am on a very similar sales call with my senior partner, DeWitt. He is a veteran of hundreds of such meetings. A wise sage. And the client asks us the same question: "Why don't you start by telling us about your firm?"

DeWitt pauses thoughtfully. He looks up, and asks, "What would you like to know about us?" Then he is silent.

(Often, we ask a question, and when there is even a small silence we ask it again in slightly different words. We can't resist filling the silence. Not DeWitt—he is very comfortable with silence. He long ago told me, "Once you've made your pitch, or you ask a question, shut up!").

The client suddenly gets more specific. "Well, we are of course broadly familiar with what you do. I'd like to understand in particular what your capabilities are in Asia, and also how you work together internally." This leads to an interactive and engaged conversation.

"I'm curious. Can you say more about 'working together internally'?" DeWitt asks. "What prompted you to raise that?" He poses some more thoughtful questions. He shares with them a few examples of our recent client assignments. These are interesting stories that highlight how we have helped similar clients.

Because of DeWitt's questions, we learn about a bad experience this company had with another consulting firm. That firm had advertised themselves as being global, but the parts did not work together well. We learn about the client's expansion plans for Asia. We find out why they are seeking outside help.

DeWitt does something else I've never forgotten. He praises me to the client. *Me*, not himself! Instead of talking about his 25 years of experience—about his commanding knowledge of the industry—he talks about how lucky he is to have me on the team. He says I'm one of their brightest young partners. One of their hardest working. Me!

The discussion is different and infinitely richer than the one I had the prior year with the telecommunications company. It is the beginning of a new relationship.

A week later the company calls DeWitt. They invite us back for more discussions. Then a proposal. DeWitt ends up working with them until he retires, eight years later. They are now my client. A client for life.

After that meeting, I was happy to carry DeWitt's bag wherever we went.

When someone says, "Tell me about your company," get them to be more specific. Ask, **"What would you like to know about us?"**

Similarly, if someone asks you, "Tell me about yourself," ask them, **"What would you like to know about me?"**

Suggestions for How to Use This Question

"What would you like to know about us?"

When someone asks us a question, we rarely ask them to clarify exactly what it is they want to know. Have you ever watched someone give a five-minute answer to the wrong question—to a question they thought they heard but which wasn't actually asked? It's painful.

Always clarify what the other person is looking for. If someone says, "Tell me about yourself," you could start with your birth—and talk for hours. Or, you could ask them what part of your background would most interest them, and start there.

When to use the question
- When you are asked a general question that could potentially require a long answer.
- When time is short and you want to be sure that your very brief answer will be right on target.

Alternative versions of the question
- "What part of my background interests you?"
- "What aspect of that situation would you like me to focus on?"
- "Before I answer that—have you had any experience with our organization in the past?"
- "What if I started by describing a couple of examples of recent work we've done for clients like you?"

Follow-up questions
- "Does that answer your question?"
- "Is there anything else you'd like me to talk about?"

3 | The Four Words

"Four words. That's all I want. Four damn words."

I'm in George's office. He's pacing furiously. Back and forth. I'm beginning to see a clear path in his carpet.

George is Vice Chancellor of a major university in the Southeast. In my book, he's tops—and I've worked with a lot of university officers.

"Calm down," I tell him. "You're going to explode. Sit."

"What's this business about the four words?" I ask him. "What do you mean?"

The story begins. Unfortunately, I've heard it before from George. He had just come from a meeting of the senior officers of the university. Nothing had changed.

"We had another one of those stupid meetings with the Chancellor. We spent three full hours with him telling us what he thinks, what he wants to do, what his priorities are, and how he feels the university is doing under his leadership."

George goes on about the Chancellor's uninterrupted ranting. I'm thinking that some folks aren't hard of hearing. They're hard of listening. That's George's Chancellor.

"If only once he would stop," George goes on, "and ask us what we think. Just once. The four words I want him to say are, '*What do you think?*'"

George is correct. Those four words, *What do you think?*, are powerful. You are seeking an opinion. The person you're talking with wants you to listen. You've heard about people who talk too much. You never heard about a person who listens too much.

One evening, Thoreau wrote in his journal: "The greatest compliment was paid to me today. Someone asked me what I thought and actually attended to my answer."

You cannot put on a pair of ice skates for the first time without looking a bit ridiculous. The art of listening can also be very slippery. Those four words George refers to are an excellent start. Ask, "What do you think about this?" Or, "How do you feel about that?"

The list of questions like this could go on. They are what we call open-ended questions. They can't be answered with a simple *yes* or *no*. They require an explanatory response.

Then you listen. You listen intently. It's what the Quakers call *devout listening*.

This may seem counterintuitive, but asking questions and then listening put you in control of the conversation. Because your questions require an answer, you are in the position of power. Good listeners are not only popular everywhere, but after awhile, they learn a thing or two.

I was reminded of all this the other day. I came across a caricature of Franklin Delano Roosevelt in one of my old files. He's leaning on his cane, bent markedly forward, listening intently to two men, obviously homeless, who appear to have stopped him somewhere.

I can't remember where I found the picture, but it's a priceless treasure. One of the men is small and scrappy-looking. His hands are in his pockets and he's leaning right into Roosevelt's face.

The other man is larger and older. He's wearing an ancient, ragged coat and is unshaved.

Roosevelt's regular grey fedora is somewhat smashed as always. He is bent far forward. It appears he is asking them what they think. He is attentive to every word that is being said to him. The caption underneath the caricature reads: "He knows how to ask how we feel."

What do you think?—four potent and irresistible words. What we know is that the need to be heard turns out to be one of the most powerful motivating forces in human nature. People want to be heard!

Studies are quite clear that we care most about people who listen to us. People crave two things above all else. They seek appreciation and they want someone to listen to them.

There is nothing more potent than these four words: *What do you think?*

By the way, the story about George has a happy ending. The Chancellor ran for office and was elected Governor of the state. George was selected to succeed him as Chancellor. Oh, one thing more. Don't even try to guess. It's a real story but I've successfully changed the names.

Develop your reputation as a great listener. Draw others out and show you care about them by asking, **"What do you think?"**

Suggestions for How to Use This Question

"What do you think?"

"Many a man would rather you heard his story than granted his request," wrote Philip Stanhope, the Fourth Earl of Chesterfield. Make those around you feel heard by asking the superb question: *What do you think?* You will open up a floodgate and become a sponge soaking up information.

Then listen. Listen aggressively. Listen attentively. Listen to the silence. Listen with your eyes. Listen!

You may not like what you hear when you ask the question. That's the risk you take. Just remember the seeds of progress are rooted in the unhappy person. It's the pebble in the shoe that causes you to take notice.

When to use the question
- Whenever you are discussing a dilemma or planning a course of future action.
- After you have shared your views or presented a proposal.
- When someone comes to you with a problem.

Alternative versions of the question
- "I value your opinion. Can I get your reaction to this?"
- "Would you be willing to share your views?"

Follow-up questions
- "What has influenced your thinking about this the most?"
- "Are there any other perspectives I ought to be aware of?"

4 | When the Sale Is Stuck

Dean Kamen is an extraordinary inventor. He has more than 100 patents to his name. He developed an insulin pump, a portable kidney dialysis machine, an electric wheelchair, and dozens of other innovations. He's backed by the wealthiest, brightest venture capitalists in the world. Few can match his record of success.

It's December 2001. Kamen is launching a new product that he says will completely revolutionize transportation around the world. He has been working on it in absolute secrecy for a decade.

It is the Segway, a battery-powered personal transportation device. The market? Six billion people. It is heralded with tremendous fanfare. In anticipation of its unveiling, *Newsweek* predicts it will be one of the most important inventions of the century.

Kamen claims that within a year, his spanking new factory will be churning out 10,000 Segways a week, with a price tag of nearly $5,000 each. According to *Wired* magazine, Kamen figured that "Executives at companies like FedEx and American Express would behold his high-tech superscooter and wonder how they'd managed all these years without it."

Actually, the factory ended up shipping about 10 Segways a week, not 10,000. A decade later, 50,000 have been sold rather than the tens of millions that were predicted.

Ride a Segway to work? To school? Not really. People had cars, buses, trains—and their two feet. No one felt a need that had to be fulfilled by an electric, upright scooter. Individuals didn't. Corporations didn't. Governments didn't.

Segway could not affirmatively answer the first question that determines whether someone will buy: *Does the buyer have a significant problem or opportunity that the solution addresses?*

No need? No sale.

Nearly 25 years earlier, on April 17, 1977, President Jimmy Carter is on national television. He gives a dramatic speech about the energy crisis.

He explains that Middle Eastern nations have raised the price of oil. The United States is dangerously dependent on foreign energy supplies. He asks Americans to sacrifice, to conserve. Shaking his fist, he calls the challenge "the moral equivalent of war."

Carter is absolutely right about the energy crisis. He is prescient, ahead of his time. But after the speech, his popularity plummets. The public does not buy his message, his plea. Not at all. Some even mock him. Why?

In 1977, Americans didn't see that they were responsible for the energy problem. They perceived it as caused by foreign suppliers of crude, as well as the big energy companies and large corporations. It wasn't their *personal* issue.

The public refused to buy President Carter's energy program because he could not affirmatively answer the second question that determines whether someone will buy: *Does the buyer own the problem?* The buyer must be able to take action. They must feel responsible—and, in an organization, empowered by their leadership to deal with the problem.

No responsibility and ownership? No sale.

During the 1970s, when Carter was president, a high-fidelity revolution was sweeping living rooms across the country. The development of the transistor, and then the integrated microchip, laid the foundation for a new generation of stereo equipment. Speaker companies like Bose began manufacturing truly superb speakers that vastly enhanced the listening experience.

Consumers loved these improvements. Soon, even college dorm rooms sported great-sounding turntables, amplifiers, and speakers. This quality explosion put previous generations of equipment to shame.

Stereophiles were now very, very satisfied with their listening experience.

Then, someone had the bright idea of Quadraphonic sound. That's right, instead of two speakers there would be four, with four distinct sound channels. If stereo sounded like a live performance, Quadraphonic sound would be like sitting in the middle of a performance stage with the players on all four sides. Huh?

Quadraphonic sound was a humongous flop. It was expensive. There were almost no recordings that could take advantage of it. And most important, consumers were highly satisfied with their already-great stereo equipment. The Quadraphonic audio system soon joined the dustbin with the Edsel car and 3-D glasses.

Quadraphonic sound could not affirmatively answer the third question that determines whether someone will buy: *Does the buyer have a healthy dissatisfaction with current offerings or with the rate of their improvement?*

No dissatisfaction? No sale.

Dubai Ports World's acquisition of British company P&O in 2005 illustrates the perils of failing to meet the fourth condition for someone to buy: *Trust* that you are the right person for the job.

Dubai Ports World is owned by the government of Dubai, which is part of the United Arab Emirates. P&O had the contracts to manage port operations in 22 major U.S. ports around the country. Even though P&O was a non-U.S. company, no one raised any objections to their management of such important national assets. The company was largely British-owned, and Britain is a staunch U.S. ally. Dubai Ports World was a different story, however.

Politicians quickly picked up on the fact that many U.S. ports would soon be under the management—albeit indirectly—of a Middle Eastern government. The acquisition came under fierce attack. There was fear-mongering about terrorists infiltrating the United States. Dubai Ports World's potential ownership of the port management contracts was portrayed as an extraordinary risk to national security. The U.S. Congress threatened to block the deal. It was a *cause célèbre* in the Capitol.

Under enormous pressure, Dubai Ports World gave in and eventually sold P&O's U.S. port management business to a U.S. company.

Dubai Ports World could not affirmatively answer the fourth question that determines if someone will buy: *Does the buyer trust that you are the best person for the job?*

No trust? No sale.

No matter what the circumstances, when you are trying to convince someone to buy, these four conditions must exist. You might be selling a service to a corporation or, perhaps, presenting a proposal for a new initiative to your boss. It doesn't matter.

When the sale is stalled, you must ask:

Does the buyer have a significant problem or opportunity that the solution addresses? (Why would they hire you to solve a problem they don't think exists, or buy a product that doesn't address a distinct need?)

Does the buyer own the problem? (Can they take action? Are they responsible? If not, you're talking to the wrong person.)

Does the buyer have a healthy dissatisfaction with current offerings or with their rate of improvement? (People will buy only when there is a gap between current performance or current offerings and their desires).

Does the buyer trust that you are the best person for the job? (I can have a problem, I can own that problem and be empowered to act, and I can have a healthy dissatisfaction with current offerings—but if I don't trust *you* or your *company* to do the job, there won't be a sale.)

If you want to sell anything, you must determine whether these four conditions exist. In the end section of this book you will find a series of additional questions to ask a potential buyer. These will help you determine whether it's a "yes" or "no" to each of these conditions.

A sale—of a service, a product, or an idea—requires an investment of scarce time and resources. You must be determined and commited. Before you exhaust yourself trying to get the sale, you must ask the question, **"Are they ready to buy?"**

Suggestions for How to Use This Question

"Are they ready to buy?"

Have you heard this before? "We talk and talk but nothing happens. They won't get off the stick and buy!"

When people are ready to buy, it is a delightful experience. They reach out toward you. They relish the interaction. But they won't buy your product, your service, or your idea if the four conditions have not been met.

Condition 1: Is there a problem or opportunity? Ask the person questions such as: "What is this costing you right now?" "If you don't fix this problem, what will the consequences be?" "What do you think this opportunity is worth?" "Is this one of your highest priorities?"

Condition 2: Does the person "own" the problem? Ask them questions such as: "Who owns this problem?" "Are you responsible for fixing this?" "Who would authorize an expenditure to address this?" "Who needs to be involved in a solution to this issue?"

Condition 3: Does the buyer have a healthy dissatisfaction with the current offering or the rate of improvement? Ask them: "Is this a minor irritant or something you're truly fed up with?" "What would you say is missing?" "Why do you feel that *now* is the time to put extra resources against this?" "How effective have your own efforts been to address this?"

Condition 4: Does the buyer trust you and believe you're the best alternative they have? Ask questions such as: "What other solutions are you looking at?" "How do you feel about our capabilities in this area?" "What concerns do you have about us or our approach?"

5 | Mission Isn't Important. It's Everything

Years of helping to solve problems have taught me that when you listen effectively and empathetically, it shows you care. And until people believe you care, they won't fully engage with you.

I am sitting with Rick Haber, who is the CEO of Life Health. It's a $2-billion health-care corporation. This is our regular monthly coaching meeting.

Life Health is a large not-for-profit medical center. The only other hospital in the area is St. Frances. It is a much smaller hospital, located in the wealthiest area of the city.

"I'm making an intensive drive to take over St. Frances," Haber tells me. "They have the largest cardiac program in the region and several dozen top heart specialists. I need to have them in my camp. It's the one area where we have a void. I'll take over the whole hospital if I need to."

"I can see where you're coming from, Rick," I reply. "You're an ambitious guy. Because of your drive and persistence, Life Health has become the market leader in this town. Can you remind me," I ask him, "what the mission of Life Health is?"

"That's easy. I talk to my staff about it all the time. It is to offer the most effective program in vital health maintenance and illness prevention and to deliver the most caring and responsive treatments available at the lowest cost possible." I pause and let it sink in. Then I ask Rick, "How would this takeover further your mission statement? Your core purpose?"

"Well," Rick begins. Then he pauses.

"Well, I just saw an opportunity that I could move in on. You know, I'm a pretty aggressive guy." My ears perk up. Whenever I hear the word "just," an alarm goes off. (I'm reminded that Harry Emerson Fosdick said that a person wrapped up in himself makes a pretty small package.)

"Tell me, Rick, where in that mission statement does it indicate that hijacking the cardiac care of St. Frances Hospital is what your mission is all about? You're going to kill them. They'll end up getting dismantled when it's over."

"What are you saying?" he asks.

"I'm not saying, I'm asking," I tell him.

Then I stop talking. I am quiet. It is a World Series silence—like what happens when the visiting team has scored eight runs in the first inning.

I say it again: "Rick, I'm asking what your mission is and how this idea will further it. Is it consistent with what you stand for?"

He doesn't have to answer—I can see it in his face. Rick knows that taking over the cardiac program from St. Frances has nothing to do with meeting Life Health's mission. He knows that even without the cardiac program, they'd still be the dominant force in the marketplace.

"Rick," I add, "we both know that bigger isn't better—better is better."

Mission is everything. It is your true north. When someone is making a big move—a significant decision—check to see if it is consistent with who they are. Ask: **"How will this further your mission and goals?"**

Suggestions for How to Use This Question

"How will this further your mission and goals?"

Our mission and goals are absolutely at the heart of who we are and who we want to be. This is true at both an institutional and personal level. Yet, we often stray from them. We get engrossed in our day-to-day lives, and we lose sight of the forest for the trees. It happens because it is very human to be drawn into things that fulfill our hunger for achievement, wealth, power, and fame. But these don't often nurture our hearts and souls.

When to use the question
- When you see someone doing things that are inconsistent with their core mission.
- When someone is making a decision to invest significant time and resources in a new direction.
- When you suspect the other person has not thought through what their mission and goals really are.

Alternative versions of the question
- "Can you remind me of your mission and goals?"
- "Is this consistent with your values and beliefs?"

Follow-up questions
- "Why or why not?"
- "Are there other ideas or initiatives you're considering that would also support your mission—which also merit consideration?"

6 | Get Out of Your Cave

Just imagine. You have been robbed of your freedom. You can no longer experience the warm glow of sunshine. Your comfortable house is gone.

Instead, you live in a totally dark cave. It is dreadfully dank. The temperature never rises above 55 degrees.

For just a moment, entertain this idea and engage in what Coleridge called "that willing suspension of disbelief."

Just imagine. You have been chained inside that cave all of your life, facing an inner wall. Behind you is a bonfire. It casts its light onto the wall. Because of the chains, you cannot turn and look at the source of the light. You can only look at the wall in front of you.

You spend your days watching shadows projected on the wall by people and things passing in front of the fire that's behind you. The shadows dance and move. You ascribe meaning to these shadows. You interpret their movements. You guess at who is casting them. The shadows are as close as you ever get to viewing the reality outside your dim corner of the cave.

What conclusions about life do you draw, based on seeing these shadows? You can only see projections of reality against the cave wall, not the real thing. Are you aware of how poor your perception really is? How little you understand about what's going on in the world, chained as you are to the wall?

A bizarre, creepy scenario? Or is this an accurate metaphor for how limited our true understanding of life around us is?

The ancient Greek philosopher Socrates describes this as the "Allegory of the Cave." You find it in Plato's *Dialogues*. The *Dialogues* are a series of conversations between Plato and his old teacher, Socrates. Socrates says a philosopher is like a prisoner who is freed from the cave and can now see reality as it truly is.

In a sense, *power questions* are our tool for helping to see the true reality around us instead of shadowy representations of it. Your spouse describes an incident involving one of your children. Is this description objective? A co-worker presents an investment proposal in an area you are not deeply knowledgeable about. How accurate is the assessment?

In both cases you are really seeing only the shadows—you are being given a filtered and biased view of what the other person thinks has happened or will happen.

We are, in essence, no different from the prisoners who are chained to the wall of the cave in Socrates's allegory. We experience life through filters.

Socrates lived in ancient Greece. He was a master at asking power questions. Instead of lecturing, he taught by posing his students a series of thought-provoking questions. Through these, he engaged his students' minds in the learning process. He uncovered their assumptions. He slowly but surely got to the heart of the issue.

Socrates would start a class by asking "What is virtue?" or "What is good?" We use these words all the time. But do we really know what they mean? Today, many universities around the world use the "Socratic Method" in their teaching—one of the most famous of these is Harvard Business School.

Socrates summed up this method very clearly. He said, "The highest form of Human Excellence is to question oneself and others."

Socrates was a vocal critic of Athenian society and government. He was eventually sentenced to death for his perceived attacks on the ruling classes. Without a struggle, he drank a cup of poison hemlock. It gradually reached his heart and he died, leaving his enduring reputation as one of the greatest philosophers in history.

Socrates surely lived his life attuned to his oft-quoted statement, "The unexamined life is not worth living."

You can use the Socratic method to great effect in your day-to-day work and personal life. How can you be more Socrates-like? First, start with questions rather than statements, assertions, or commands.

Consider these examples:

Instead of: "We need to improve our customer service!"

Try: "How would you assess our customer service levels today?" or, "How is our service impacting our customer retention?"

Instead of: "You know, if you don't get a job this summer, we're not paying you an allowance."

Try: "What ideas do you have for what you'd like to do this summer?" or, "I'm interested to hear about how your job search is going. What are you looking into?"

Instead of: "I'm fed up with your anger."

Try: "When you get angry, how do you think it affects your relationships with the people closest to you?"

Second, ask *fundamental* questions about the things that everyone else takes for granted—questions that will, perhaps surprise others.

For example, someone at work says, "We need more innovation." Ask, "Can you describe what innovation means to you?" When there is a call for more teamwork, ask, "What do *you* mean when you say 'teamwork'?"

You're with a friend who says they want more work-life balance. Ask this friend, "What is work-life balance for you?" Someone says, "I don't trust him." You might respond, "Why not? What is *trust* for you in this situation?"

Questions like these will result in deep, rewarding conversations that engage others and make them think. You'll develop a reputation as a wise shepherd—a leader who gently moves people in the right direction rather than imposing your views on them.

Adopt the Socratic mindset and get out of your cave! Question assumptions. Question the very definition of words that others take for granted. Use questions to launch those around you on an invigorating journey of learning and discovery.

Suggestions for Using the Socratic Approach

When you adopt the Socrates mindset, you approach almost every conversation differently. Here is a contrast that will help you understand this mindset:

Instead of:	You:
Telling	Ask thought-provoking questions
Being the expert	Invite others to contribute expertise
Controlling knowledge	Help draw out others' experiences
Assuming meaning	Ask about the meaning of words
Mandating solutions	Solicit solutions from others
Showing how smart *you* are	Show others how smart *they* are
Analyzing	Synthesize and look at the big picture

"Remember that there is nothing stable in human affairs; therefore avoid undue elation in prosperity, or undue depression in adversity."

—Socrates, 469–399 B.C.

7 | Begin at the Beginning

"Jay had to borrow the money. I didn't have a single penny I could contribute."

I'm having lunch with Rich DeVos at the 1913, the toniest restaurant in Grand Rapids, Michigan. It would rival anything in New York. Rich is having his favorite lunch, a bowl of chili. Actually, two bowls of chili.

We're getting fantastic service and I'm not surprised. Rich owns the restaurant. As a matter of fact, he owns the hotel and the restaurant in it. He also owns the Marriott across the street and a few more blocks in downtown Grand Rapids.

He's one of the most extraordinary men I've ever met. Modest. Generous. A roaring patriot. And a motivating speaker who cannonballs you out of your chair, clapping and cheering.

He's an inspiration. His life is one long creation and celebration.

Oh, one thing more. Forbes has listed his net worth at several billion dollars. That's a "B."

Rich is co-founder of Amway with his high school friend and army buddy, Jay Van Andel. It was a mystical bonding. Even after both retired, they were in contact with each other every day.

Today, the corporation is a $20-billion operation. There are 3 million Amway distributors in 80 countries around the world.

Talk about inspiring. I heard him once give a rousing 30-minute presentation. On the spot, I wanted to become an Amway representative! What Rich is proudest of is that he has made so many men and women millionaires. He says there are hundreds of them.

"Rich," I say to him, "it's a fascinating story of what you've done. Tell me, how did you get started?"

"Begin at the beginning," the King of Hearts said to Alice, "and go on till you come to the end."

What follows is an account that reads like a fairy tale, but it's all true.

"Jay and I didn't have time for college. We wanted to be entrepreneurs. Although at the time, I'm not certain we knew what the word meant.

"We get out of the army and we know we want to go into business together and for ourselves. We are convinced that's the American dream.

"We start in the charter airplane business. But that doesn't work out at all. So what is next, we wondered."

(I'm reminded that you learn from experience, and mistakes give you experience. Winston Churchill said success is to go from one failure to another failure without losing your enthusiasm.)

"Right after the charter airplane failure, Jay hears about Nutrilite. That's a food enhancer. We do some checking. We learn we could become distributors.

"So we begin by wanting to buy a sales kit and samples. That will take 50 dollars. But we don't have that much between us. Jay has to borrow the 50 dollars to get us into business. I didn't even have enough money to contribute a penny.

"Well, over the years, the business really grows. Jay and I eventually have 5,000 Nutrilite distributors who work for us. We want a broader product range. In 1959 we found the American Way Association. It later was renamed Amway. There was no one like us."

Rich goes on to tell me about the growth of Amway. It became more than just a distribution company. It was a way of life, an organization where, with motivation and hard work, anyone could succeed regardless of their background.

Rich and I spend nearly three hours at the luncheon table. But how his company got started is the real story. I find the question I first asked Rich leads me on wondrous, uncharted journeys— "How did you get started?"

I ask that very same question (How did you get started?) of Mary Kay Ash, founder of Mary Kay Cosmetics. What a story hers is—she was a single mother who had to quickly find a way to support her infant son.

And there was Cal Turner, Jr. (Dollar General) who first started by selling a pair of bloomers. (Yes—bloomers!) There are dozens and dozens of other stories just like that.

As for Rich DeVos, he was born one of God's originals. In the canons of corporate life, he is rife for beatitude.

"How did you get started?" is a question even the most celebrated, powerful, or wealthy person cannot resist. But try it with anyone you meet along the way—it's also a question for a friend, colleague, or stranger. The stories that unfold will be surprisingly exciting.

Follow the dictum of the King of Hearts. Begin at the beginning. "How did you get started" will lead you on a wondrous path where golden nuggets of conversation and information are ready for you to mine.

You can truly engage with someone, draw them out, and learn their story by asking **"How did you get started?"**

Suggestions for How to Use This Question

"How did you get started?"

Of all the questions you might ask, what's best about this one is the joy, passion, and inspiration it brings to both you and the teller. *How did you get started* provides a many-splendored array of stories. Each one is precious, full of joy (and, at times, heartbreak along the way). And often some precious laughter.

In asking this question, you will find men and women who live life with a playful curiosity. They are willing to risk it all, to roll the dice. They are not afraid to go out on a limb, because they know that's where the fruit is.

When you ask, "How did you get started?" you also help recognize the ordinary as extraordinary. Every friend, colleague, or even stranger has a story that is dear to them. How they chose their profession. How they met their spouse. That serendipitous trip to Los Angeles, where they ended up settling down. When these stories are shared, a connection is created.

When to use the question
- Anytime, to invite someone to share how they got started in their career—or in any other part of their lives.

Alternative versions of the question
- *Of a couple:* "How did you two meet and end up together?"
- *Of an artist or musician:* "Who taught you? How did you learn your craft?"
- *Of anyone:* "Where did you grow up? And how did you end up in . . . ?"

Follow-up questions
- "How did you decide to do that at the time?"
- "What was the toughest lesson you had to learn?"
- "If that had fallen through . . . what do you think would have happened?"

8 | Start Over

"You're not only smoking it," he says. "You're inhaling." He isn't smiling.

I am talking with Allan Favort about a gift to his alma mater. I know from everything he has told me, and from his gifts in the past, he has great passion for his university. I also know that he has the high financial capacity to make a major gift. And he knows I know!

Because I am so certain of his dedication to his alma mater, I don't waste any time getting into our discussion. I greet him and launch right into it.

"Allan, I know how much you love the university. I'd like you to make a gift of a million dollars to go to the College of Engineering where you graduated. I know you're committed to the College and that's where your recent annual gifts have been going."

That's when he stops me in my tracks. A hand as big as a baseball mitt is in my face.

"You come busting in here and just like that, you ask me for a million bucks. And you assume I'd be interested in the College of Engineering."

The Cherokee Indians had a saying they used before going into war: "It's a good day to die." That's how I feel. Actually, I

believe the battle is over and I am being carried off on a stretcher.
I look at Allan and take a deep breath.

"I can't believe I really did that, Allan." (What was I thinking?
I know you're supposed to take time to gain rapport. And then as
subtly as the landing of a butterfly, you can begin exploring to find
the right motivations.). "I'm embarrassed, Allan. I thought I knew
you so well I just went dashing in. I'm so sorry for my thoughtless-
ness. Forgive me."

Then, I pick up my briefcase and my coat and leave. I don't
even say goodbye. I just close the door and leave.

About 20 seconds later, I knock on the door. I open it a crack.

"Hi, Allan. Can I come in for a few minutes? I have something
very special to talk with you about. It's about the university. I think
you are going to find this terribly exciting." I add: "And by the
way, do you mind if we start completely over?" Allan smiles, and
nods his head without speaking.

Then I do what I should have done to begin with. I chat, ob-
serve, and begin asking questions. Most of all, I encourage Allan to
talk. I discreetly try to work the key in the lock.

Here's what I hear. After some artful prying, it turns out Allan
isn't interested at all in making a gift to the College of Engineering.
He's interested in the theater program at the university.

He tells me: "I guess no one but my wife knows this but when
I entered the university, I was a drama major. I wanted to be an
actor. Fortunately, I switched to engineering—and the world was
saved from having a very bad actor.

"If I am going to make a gift, and mind you, I'm not saying
I will—I'd be happy to talk some more about that crazy amount of
money you asked me for before you took off so abruptly."

We talk and talk.

Finally, he says, "You know that theater program we're talking
about? (Actually, he did all the talking. I just inserted a question
now and then.) I suppose if you give me a couple of extra years,
I could probably make a gift of a million bucks."

I'm reciting Psalms.

It may feel awkward, but it's a bold, gutsy strategy to restart a conversation from scratch. It could be with someone at work or a family member at home. When you get off on the wrong foot, ask, **"Do you mind if we start over?"**

Suggestions for How to Use This Question

"Do you mind if we start over?"

Be careful not to jump right into a request without probing and asking questions. It is comparable to pushing a non-swimmer into the deep end. They may not come up for air. And they may take you down with them.

People are forgiving. They want to have a great conversation with you. Asking, "Do you mind if we start over?" will disarm the other person and make them smile. That smile will ease the way to a new beginning.

When to use the question
- When a conversation gets off to a very bad start.
- If you get into an unproductive, emotionally charged argument with a friend or family member.

Alternative versions of the question
- "I've gotten off on the wrong foot. Do you mind if I begin again? I haven't done this justice."
- "Can we step back from this? What *should* we be talking about?"

Follow-up questions
- "Thanks. Do you mind if I ask you a question?"
- "The reason I'd like to start over is that I put my foot in my mouth. Can I give it a second try?"

9 | You Can Overcome Anything If You Understand *Why*

I read the job description again. Good grief! *Where do they come up with this stuff?*

I am sitting at a large conference table, high atop one of the tallest buildings in Manhattan. I'm about to reconvene the group. Sitting with me are 18 of the most seasoned bankers in the world. They are among the senior account executives for a global financial powerhouse.

They can arrange huge credit facilities. Ensure financing for a transformational takeover. Move billions of dollars around the globe in seconds. The bank's revenues, profits, and share price are heavily dependent on the performance of this elite group of individuals.

But they are frustrated. Stymied by internal bureaucracy. Pressed by shareholders who want even greater returns on capital. Monitored by measurement systems that record their every move. Hemmed in by metrics that make long-term investment in relationships difficult.

I am helping them redefine their role and develop a client-centric rather than product-driven approach. These powerful executives are the vanguard meant to be ushering in a new era of client focus.

They put their mission at the top of a sleek PowerPoint slide. The headline says, "Our Mission." It contains many elegant words like *maximize, align, synergize, profitable,* and *multi-faceted.* But the mission that's been defined doesn't sound client-centric. No, it sounds about as "client first" as the turkey is "first" on Thanksgiving. In plain English, it reads something like this:

Our mission is to sell, as often as possible, all of the bank's services to our key clients.

It's not inspiring or distinctive.

It is at odds with the genuine enthusiasm this group of 18 über-bankers has for serving their clients while acting as trusted advisors who always put their clients' interests first.

"When people ask *how,*" I tell them, "they stay busy and always have a job. They become good managers. But if they ask *why* they become more than that. They start to lead, not just manage."

I turn to my audience. "Shall we start up?" Heads nod.

"Let's talk about your mission and your role. I have a question: *Why do you do what you do?*"

I wait. I do not repeat the question, or elaborate on what I mean. Its meaning is clear to them.

The room becomes still.

Then, slowly, heads start nodding. Several of them begin to smile knowingly.

"That's a good question," one of them says.

I look around the room. Gradually, the dam is bursting. We go around the table. One by one they began to talk enthusiastically about how important their role is. How they love helping their clients grow their businesses and thrive in their careers.

"I do this because I make such a big difference to my clients," says one.

"I like having an impact," says another.

"This is the best job at the bank. The toughest, but also the best."

"I feel like I'm on the deck of an aircraft carrier, scanning the horizon to see if there's an opportunity to help."

"I bring it all together for clients."

"I'm the one who is ultimately accountable for the entire relationship, and I make it happen."

"I love the deep, personal relationships I build with my clients."

I am smiling. The room lights up with their passion for the *why* of their work. Their energy is palpable. I now see what allows them to surmount the bureaucratic hurdles of their global organization. I am reminded of what Friederich Nietzsche said: "He who has a *why* to live can bear almost any *how*."

Twenty minutes later we have the basic elements of their new mission. It's not a mission based on selling more products and making "superior returns." No, it's one founded on helping clients achieve their most important goals. On using the unique strengths of their organizations. It is motivating and distinctive.

The mood in the room is transformed. The dead hand of internal meetings and endless reports is pushed aside. In its place is excitement and passion for the real job.

When you're trying to define an organizational role, to restore a sense of purpose and pride, or just understand what makes people tick, ask: **"Why do you do what you do?"**

Suggestions for How to Use This Question

"Why do you do what you do?"

We do things for many different reasons. But when you put "should" in front of those reasons, you can be certain all the pleasure and excitement will be soon drained away. You will not find passion associated with the word *should*. No one gets excited about *should*.

In contrast, when you unveil the true *why* of someone's work and actions, you will find passion, energy, and excitement.

When to use the question
- When you want to understand what motivates and drives the other person.
- To help reenergize other people about their vocation.

Alternative versions of the question
- "What are the most exciting parts of your job/of what you do? Why?"
- "What are you most passionate about in your professional life? Your personal life? Why?"

Follow-up questions
- "Why are you especially passionate about that?"
- "What gets in the way of your satisfaction?"
- "What would make it even more rewarding?"

10 | In a Hushed Moment

Do you know anyone who smokes a corncob pipe? I didn't think so. Do you even know what a corncob pipe is? I didn't think so.

Well . . . Alan G. Hassenfeld smokes a corncob pipe, And it's not because he can't afford better. But the pipe isn't all that's unusual about Alan. In a few moments, you will learn more about this corporate leader, philanthropist, and world traveler.

The former Governor of Rhode Island, Bruce Sundlun, told me one day, "Alan is the most influential person in the state, one of our strongest and most effective leaders." It's not just that Alan at the time was CEO of the largest employer in the state, although that is a factor.

"He's an inspiration," says the Governor. "He leads by example. He's involved in dozens of activities that are good for the state and good for his Temple."

At age 41, Alan becomes CEO of Hasbro, the family corporation his grandfather founded. The company produces toys and games.

Hasbro grows by leaps and bounds under Alan's leadership. It now has revenues of $4 billion a year (that's a lot of toys and games) and is the juggernaut of their market. *Fortune* magazine called it one of the hundred best companies in the nation.

Alan left active involvement in Hasbro a few years ago. He remains as Chairman of the Board. I'm impressed with the company's mission: *We Are Determined to Succeed*. Alan also lives by that tenet.

I have been with him many times. On this particular evening I am writing about, we are having a leisurely dinner at the Harvard Club in Manhattan. We talk and talk.

"Hasbro more than doubled its earnings during your tenure, Alan. As CEO, how did you handle tough situations and problems?"

"I have a saying," he tells me. "It's my philosophy: 'Problems are like an ice cream cone. If you don't lick them, they cause a mess.'" (I match this with one of my own: Winners are like teabags—you never see their true strength until they're in hot water.)

He treats me to a dozen more of his sayings. It is magnificent fun.

"You have been an immense success in life," I tell Alan. "A recognized corporate leader nationally. A mover of great regard within the Jewish community locally and nationally. One of the most important spokespersons in Rhode Island. Add to that a half-dozen honorary doctorates. *What in your life has given you the greatest fulfillment?*"

It's a question I never raised before with Alan. Even with someone as facile as he is, I was certain he would have to take some time to think the question over before responding. But that isn't the case.

"It's very clear what has been most fulfilling for me," Alan tells me. "It's Hasbro Children's Hospital (in Providence). Our family put up the money for the hospital. When you see the kids we help and you talk with some of the grateful parents, it makes everything else I've done in life pale in comparison.

"You know what I like best? At Christmastime I visit every room with a present. What could possibly be more important? What could possibly give you greater joy?" Alan speaks with buoyancy and a deeply etched spirit.

The question leads to his telling me about his sponsorship of the Leadership Scholarship Program at Harvard and also at Bryant University in Smithfield, Rhode Island. Alan also provides major funding to supply clean water and assist with eliminating poverty in Sudan, Haiti, Afghanistan, Thailand, and Israel.

Alan is among the blessed ones. He seems to seize the trunk of life. He is committed to inspire others to dream more, learn more, do more, and become more.

After my simple question, he continues talking. I learn so much. There is a Russian word, *shamanstuo*—the quality of enchantment.

Then, something incredible happens. It is all a result of my question. He swears me to secrecy.

"I want to tell you something," he says. "But it has to be kept in the strictest of confidence. We'll probably announce it in the next few weeks. For now only a few know about it, and now you."

He leans closer, almost whispering. He makes certain no one is overhearing our conversation.

"We are giving what will end up being close to $100 million to a project in Manhattan. It will take the city and perhaps the country completely by storm. It is one of the most exciting and most needed programs in the city. Just thinking about it gives me shivers."

You may recall that I initially asked Alan, "What in your life has given you the greatest fulfillment?" That early question opens up a whole new area of Alan's life I hadn't before known about. It's a vein that leads to a mother lode. And because it's such an engaging question, it also provides a confidential conversation I would not otherwise have been privy to.

Try this question with your friends, colleagues, and family. Ask them, **What in your life has given you the greatest fulfillment?** Then sit back. Just listen. You will uncover a treasure chest of conversational gems.

Suggestions for How to Use This Question

"What in your life has given you the greatest fulfillment?"

A sense of fulfillment is different from a feeling of accomplishment or happiness. Fulfillment comes from achieving your hopes and dreams. It reflects a state of completeness or wholeness. It's when you have a sense of deep satisfaction.

When you ask someone about what fulfills them, it opens the door to exploring something that is invariably very special to that person. It creates a powerful connection, like sharing a relaxed meal or spending an intimate evening together.

When to use the question
- To build a more personal connection with someone at work or in a professional setting.
- To get to know any of your friends and family better.

Alternative versions of the question
- "What in your life gives you your greatest sense of satisfaction?"
- "What is the most fulfilling . . . (relationship, experience, job, etc.) that you've ever had?"
- "What experience affected you the most in your life?"

Follow-up questions:
- "Say more about that. What was especially fulfilling about it?"
- "Is there anything else that has also been deeply fulfilling for you?"

11 | Is This the Best You Can Do?

It is late 1983. Apple Computer is about to announce the Macintosh. Its innovative features—a mouse you move with your hand, a graphic user interface, and more—will shape the world of personal computers for decades to come.

Let me set the scene.

Steve Jobs loved to introduce his new, innovative products with a roaring media splash. No one could rival his sense of drama—the roll of drums, the trumpets signaling a new day.

Now I want you to think back to Super Bowl XVIII, 1984. Very few will remember who played. Even fewer, the score.

But no one who saw it will forget the Apple commercial. A woman in a track suit races into an auditorium filled with drone-like people. She hurls a sledgehammer into a giant movie screen that shows the talking head of an authoritarian dictator. That commercial is now nearly two decades old. It won all sorts of awards. The video of it has become a cult thing, still causing a buzz.

At Apple headquarters, in the months leading up to the launch and the commercial, the staff is working at a frenzied pace.

Sleepless nights. Lunches at the worktable. Steve Jobs is relentlessly prowling the hallways.

"Make it better. Even better," Jobs exhorts his product developers.

Jobs always demanded that every Apple product be exceptional. His zeal to produce "insanely great" products was a powerful, unrelenting force during his two long stints as Apple chief executive. Extraordinarily, he revolutionized not one but five industries: desktop computing, music, cell phones, retailing, and even cartoon animation (through Pixar).

Let me tell you what happened one day. He visited the cubicle of the Macintosh's chief engineer. "Boot it up," he tells him. He refers to the working model of the soon-to-be revolutionary new desktop computer that sits on the engineer's desk.

It takes several minutes to start up. That's because it needs to test its memory, initialize the operating system, and perform other start-up tasks.

"You have to make it boot faster," Jobs tells him. He walks away.

Weeks later, after working tirelessly to improve the computer's efficiency, the engineer proudly shows Jobs how they have managed to slightly decrease the boot time.

"Is that the best you can do?" Jobs asks him. He turns around and brusquely leaves.

After many sleepless nights, the Macintosh team manages to shave a few more seconds off. When they meet again with Jobs, he is still not satisfied. But instead of berating them further, he simply stares at the prototype with a far-off look in his eyes. He is lost in thought. When the engineer starts to explain a few ways they might be able to further improve the boot time, Jobs interrupts.

"I've been thinking about this," he says, his voice rising with excitement. "How many people are going to be using the Macintosh? A million? No, in a few years, I bet 5 million people will be booting up their Macintoshes at least once a day. Well, let's say you can shave 10 seconds off the boot time. Multiply that by 5 million users and that's 50 million seconds, every single day. Over a year, that's dozens of lifetimes. So if you make it boot 10 seconds faster, you've saved at least a dozen lives."

Jobs concludes by saying, "So it's worth it to cut another 10 seconds!"

They don't think it's possible. But the Macintosh engineers are inspired—no, driven—by Job's fervent desire to save humanity from billions of wasted seconds. They recommit themselves to the effort, and within days they successfully shorten the boot time by another 10 seconds.

Steve Jobs passed away on October 5th, 2011 at the age of 56. Because of his unparalleled innovation and drive, Apple became the most valuable technology company in the world. Thanks to Jobs, the question, "Is this the best we can do?" infuses its corporate culture.

How many of the people around you at work are actually doing their best?

Eleven years before the launch of the Macintosh, Secretary of State Henry Kissinger picks up the phone to call his special assistant, Winston Lord, into his office.

Lord is a man of considerable intellect. He will go on to become ambassador to China and also a U.S. congressman. Kissinger has a straightforward, even routine request: He asks Lord to write a presidential foreign policy report. Lord knows his boss demands the best from everyone who works for him, but even he is unprepared for what happens next.

(Perhaps Lord forgot that Kissinger's extraordinary thesis as an undergraduate at Harvard was entitled "The Meaning of History" and was no less than 377 pages long!).

Lord himself tells the story:

> I developed a good draft of the policy report, and turned it in to Kissinger. He calls me in the next day and says, "Is this the best you can do?" I say, "Henry, I thought so, but I'll try again." So I go back in a few days with another draft. He calls me in the next

day and he says, "Are you sure this is the best you can do?" I say, "Well, I really thought so. I'll try one more time." Anyway, this goes on eight times, eight drafts; each time he says, "Is this the best you can do?" So I go in there with a ninth draft, and when he calls me in the next day and asks me that same question, I really get exasperated and I say, "Henry, I've beaten my brains out—this is the ninth draft. I know it's the best I can do: I can't possibly improve one more word." He then looks at me and says, "In that case, now I'll read it."*

Kissinger was a taskmaster. But there is no question that those who worked for him produced the best, highest-quality work of their lives. Small wonder. They were a crack, superb team. But most important was Kissinger's admonishment—"Is this the best you can do?"

This is an exceptional power question. Use it sparingly and carefully—it can drive someone nearly mad. But use it. You will help others achieve things they did not believe possible.

When you want to push someone to exercise their abilities to the maximum—when you need their best possible work, ask: **"Is this the best you can do?"**

Source: www.gwu.edu/~nsarchiv/coldwar/interviews/episode-15/lord1 .html.

Suggestions for How to Use This Question

"Is this the best you can do?"

You should reserve this question for occasions when it is especially desirable for someone to do their very best and push themselves to their strained and stretched limits.

Often, we settle for mediocrity when we do need our best. Mediocrity is the enemy of greatness. Like Gresham's law: "Bad money drives out good." Companies give lousy customer service, yet they wonder why they are losing market share. College students slide by with half-hearted efforts, but want to be offered the plum jobs when they graduate.

Apathy is rampant.

This question can spur the other person to greater heights and make them focus on what their *best* really is.

When to use the question
- When you've asked someone at work to complete a task or project for you.
- When trying to get a child to raise their effort to the next level.
- Best of all, when you're working on a project, whatever it is—a writing assignment, responding to an RFP, preparing a vision statement for a company, or even working in your garden. Ask yourself, "Is this really the best I can do?"

Alternative versions of the question
- "Is there still room for further improvement?"
- "In what ways could this be even better?"

Follow-up questions
- "What's stopping you?"
- "Do you think this would be worth your 'best'?"
- "What's the best part of this? What can be improved?"

12 | No Gorilla Dust

It is one of my prized possessions—a book inscribed by Richard Cornuelle. It's called *Reclaiming the American Dream*. (President Obama liked the phrase so much he used it for the title of his book.)

"To my good friend with my very best wishes." It was signed "Dick".

Well, a moment of truth. He was being very kind. We weren't really good friends, but we were close working acquaintances. You understand, don't you, the difference?

The book made an indelible impression on me—as did the author. The book took the country by storm and made the *New York Times* Best Seller list for a number of weeks. It had a freshness of energy and boldness of renewal. It ignited a spark that set the human soul on fire.

I was working on a project to find funding for college students through private banks instead of borrowing from the government. Dick Cornuelle was spearheading the effort. Working with him, I felt I heard trumpets signaling a cavalry charge.

He died recently. He was a giant, a sturdy tree reaching for the heavens. In its day, his book was somewhat shocking. But it turned out to be a new doctrine for many.

The book makes the case that any program for social improvement that is dependent on government funding is ill-advised and likely to be corrupt. He says that the government talks about brilliant results, little interference, and generous funding. (I am reminded that Hamlet assures us that the devil may assume a pleasing shape.)

Cornuelle espoused the role of individuals and voluntary non-profits. His book became the Magna Carta of individual responsibility —a secular scripture.

It was Cornuelle who coined the term *Independent Sector*. He described the way you must deal with urgent social needs without government involvement. The concept was evolutionary, but the impact would be revolutionary.

He loved to quote De Tocqueville. I am in his office one day when he pulls out a sheath of papers and reads to me how De Tocqueville claims that our country has a genius for solving problems without government involvement.

Our program for funding scholarship assistance to college students through private banking is a tremendous success. In a very short time, we enlist more than 400 banks. One of the great delights in life is achieving something that others tell you is impossible to accomplish.

Next, Cornuelle wants to take on housing for the disadvantaged. He is determined. Unwavering. Resolute, as only Cornuelle can be. Confident as a Methodist with four aces.

"I want an answer," he says to me one day. "And I want it now."

Cornuelle wants me to make an unequivocal commitment to the project.

"Are you with me on this or aren't you? I want a yes or a no." He has a way of looking right through you, penetrating into your inner soul.

But I have a problem. I love the guy and I am dedicated to his philosophy. But there is another job looming, the possibility of a move to another part of the country, and also some graduate work. I pause.

I'll tell you my response in a moment. Let me first explain about Gorilla Dust. You've heard the expression.

When two male gorillas engage in a battle, there's quite a demonstration. They circle each other, and circle again, and again.

In the process, they rake their hands in the dirt, scooping up handfuls that when thrown in the air make quite a dust storm. This is Gorilla Dust. Nothing decisive happens. The gorillas just keep circling and circling.

Cornuelle's question is the right one to ask. He wants a yes or a no. And no Gorilla Dust. He wants to know whether I want a ticket on his speeding bus.

Often when asked a direct question, the person you're calling on will throw up Gorilla Dust. They don't want to give you a direct answer. They circle around and around.

It's your job to determine whether they are on board, whether the answer is yes or no—or are they just throwing up gorilla dust. The only way to elicit a clear response is to ask a closed-ended question. *Is it yes or no?*

It's decision time.

I've got to give this evangelist of small government an answer. Do I go with him on this next adventure or do I spend the rest of my life on a thin diet of Pablum?

"Yes, yes. I'm with you all the way, Dick."

What if Cornuelle had made a statement such as: "I would like you to consider joining me on this new venture." Or asked the question, "What do you think about the possibility of working on this new program?" Or something of the sort. That would have led to a pleasant discussion but to no decisive action.

That's not what he wanted. He wanted "Is it yes or no?" This is why a closed-ended question is precisely right in certain situations.

His life was a triumph. We enjoy in this country the painstaking, hands-on work, in thought and deed, of the sector to which Cornuelle affixed the proud adjective, "independent."

When you want a clear, unequivocal answer, ask an unequivocal, closed-ended question. Ask, **"Is it a yes or a no?"**

Suggestions for How to Use This Question

"Is it a yes or a no?"

When you are trying to pin someone down on an issue, or determine their commitment, there are many ways you can ask the question. There are soft, inquiring approaches like "What would you think of . . . ?" Sometimes, you must leave no room to wiggle.

A closed-ended question is potent when you want a direct, unvarnished response. Is it a yes or a no? When asked purposely, in an appropriate way, the closed-ended question is a powerful and demanding ally to the asker.

When to use the question
- To find out whether or not someone is fully committed.
- To draw out any doubts or hesitations.

Alternative versions of the question
- "Can you commit fully to this?"
- "Are you on board or not?"
- "Can you make a final decision now?"

Follow-up questions
- "What excites you most about this?"
- "What are your biggest doubts or reservations?"

13 | Bury the Clichés

"I threw him out of my office."

"What?"

I'm with Fred, the chief executive of the North American operations of a multinational corporation. Fred was formerly the chief information officer (CIO) of one of the world's largest banks. He's had hundreds of salespeople call on him over the years.

"You name the company," he tells me. "Goldman Sachs, IBM, Accenture, McKinsey, EDS, and then every bucket shop between here and the West Coast as well. They've all tried to sell me something."

Fred is smart and tough and doesn't tolerate fools. But I have a hard time picturing him throwing someone out of his office.

"You literally kicked him out? You're kidding?"

"I'm not kidding," says Fred. "He asked *the* question."

"Which one?"

"*What keeps you up at night?*"

He continues, shaking his head: "You see, it's a terrible question. Overused. Clichéd. Stale. And worst of all, lazy. I hate lazy salespeople. At a certain point it seemed that every salesperson, banker, and consultant was asking that question. They were like lemmings. They'd come and call on me and invariably ask, 'What keeps you up at night?'

"They thought that by posing that question I would—as if by magic—immediately volunteer to tell them all about my toughest issues. Then they could say, 'Ah, we have a solution to fix that.' I started escorting them from my office."

"And it doesn't work that way with you?" I ask. (I know that it doesn't work that way with most people, but I want to understand how Fred thinks about it).

"No, it doesn't. Nor with anyone else. Look, let's get some more coffee and I'll explain why. I'll tell you what the really smart ones do that *is* effective."

Fred's executive assistant brings us two fresh cups. We move from his desk to a small sitting area with a couch, a coffee table, and an easy chair. We settle in.

I can't believe my good fortune. I'm like a 14-year-old again, listening to my cigar-smoking, cognac-sipping Uncle Morton discuss his philosophy of good living. But now, I'm going to school with the world's best instructor on how to have a great first meeting with an executive prospect.

Sir Isaac Newton, referring to his extraordinary scientific breakthroughs, said, "I stood on the shoulders of giants." I feel like Fred is lifting me onto his back, and I'm definitely going along for the ride.

"Here's why," Fred explains, "'What keeps you up at night?' is a terrible question. First, it's a shot in the dark. It doesn't demonstrate to the other person that you've done your homework, researched the organization, and thought about the issues they face. It's a question that requires zero preparation. That's why it's evidence of laziness."

I'm scribbling furiously.

"Second, if someone doesn't already know you pretty well, they are probably not going to tell you what is *really* on their mind. Teasing that out requires that you first build some trust and credibility. Come on! Think about it. Am I going to immediately share my innermost cares and concerns with some salesperson *I've never met before*? Are you kidding?

"Third—and this is especially true if you're talking to a CEO or a really senior executive—this is a problem question. At my level, I'm focused on growth and innovation, not operational problems. I have operating executives who are paid to worry about those problems. Ultimately, executives like me are paid for growth and innovation. 'What keeps you up at night?' doesn't actually help you get at the most fruitful issues."

"So, what do the smart ones ask?"

"You have to approach a meeting with me as a balancing act. You must prepare. Read my annual report. Search the web. Read my speeches. Watch the videos of me being interviewed. Review analysts' reports. Learn about my priorities and strategies before you walk in the door.

"But then—and this is really important—when you sit down in front of my desk, don't presume to know what my real issues are. Be confident, but be humble. Probe and possibly suggest, but don't walk in here and tell me what I'm concerned about."

"The great salespeople ask indirect questions that show they know their stuff. They say things like, 'Fred, how are you reacting to the merger of two of your biggest competitors? Or, 'I was intrigued by what you said at the investors conference in New York last month. How is your push into Asian markets going to impact your financial controls and risk management requirements?'

"The other day, someone had carefully read our proxy statement, and she asked me some very intelligent questions about our executive compensation plan. She wanted to know why we had made certain choices. It was an engaging discussion. She kept gently probing, asking questions. She learned a lot about what is on my mind and about my talent management and retention strategies. We were satisfied with our existing provider, and had no intention of giving her any business. But she was so artful—I believe her firm will get a project from us.

"In other words, ask me questions that implicitly show you are knowledgeable and experienced. Talk about your view of my competition, and how you think the industry is evolving. Get me involved in that dialogue. Then, I'll start to open up. Once that happens, you can be a little more direct.

"You might even say: 'Given all that we've discussed—x, y, and z—where do you wish you were making faster progress? Which of these issues are proving to be the toughest nut to crack?'"

We wrap up, and I'm beaming. In one hour I've just had a semester's course in advanced salesmanship.

"Fred, this has been terrific. And thanks for the coffee."

"I enjoyed the discussion. And by the way, you're a darned good listener. Call anytime."

The meeting reminds me that powerful individuals like to help the people in their network. They enjoy doing favors for others. Sometimes, asking a client or colleague for advice creates an opportunity for them to feel good about your relationship—and for you to learn.

When you want to understand a leader's issues, don't ask tired cliché questions like "What keeps you up at night?" Engage them in a discussion about their critical challenges. Ask about the impact of current events. Ask about the future.

Let me give a few examples that will stimulate your thinking:

- "Where will your future growth come from?"
- "How do you think your current strategy is going to change, given . . . (e.g., the success of new competitors, the rise of low-cost imports, deregulation, etc.)"
- "If you had additional resources, which initiatives would you invest them in?"
- "Sometimes a 'breakthrough' requires a 'break-with.' Are there any things you need to deemphasize or stop doing?"

- "Why have you been successful so far? How will that change in the future?"
- "Which organizational or operational capabilities do you need to strengthen in order to achieve your goals?"
- "As you think about the future of your business, what are you most excited about? What are you most concerned about?"

Don't ask lazy clichés like "What keeps you up at night?" Instead, ask informed questions about the future. Questions that capture the imagination. Questions about the other person's aspirations, priorities, and reactions to the world around them.

Other Questions That Are Clichés

"What has surprised you?"

This is a question people love to ask someone who has taken on a new job or been through a significant new experience. But there's no good answer that is honest and positive at the same time. If you're surprised about something, it implies you were naïve and didn't know what you were getting yourself into! If you say nothing has surprised you, then you risk coming across as complacent or insensitive. Barry Glassner, the President of Lewis and Clark College, put it this way in the *Wall Street Journal*:

> "If I had a thousand dollars for every time I've been asked that question—*What has surprised you?*—in the seven months I've been in my new position as a college president, I could buy a well-equipped Lexus. It's the ultimate 'gotcha' question . . . every answer is perilous."

(continued)

(continued)

Here are the questions I prefer to ask instead: "What have you been focusing on most during your first six months on the job?" or "Have you developed a longer-term agenda yet for your role?"

"What question haven't I asked?"

A well-known marketing expert calls this his killer question for wrapping up a sales call. This question-about-a-question is a patently obvious attempt to make your prospective customer a coach to you in your sales process rather than an adversary. It's a somewhat manipulative, cutesy attempt to say, "We're really on the same side of the table here . . . give me some advice on how to be a more effective salesperson!" Like "What keeps you up at night," it's also overused.

There are many more like this. They fall into the same category as the "get them saying 'yes' three times before you ask" approach that you should shun.

Here are the questions I prefer to ask instead: "Are there any issues we haven't discussed that you think are relevant to this particular challenge?" or, "Is there anyone else you think I should I talk to in order to get additional perspective on this issue?"

14 | Don't Let Anyone Steal Your Dreams

For more than 20 years, Ben Sampson put in 60-hour workweeks. He climbed the corporate ladder, assuming positions of greater and greater responsibility and authority.

The name Ben Sampson may not be familiar to you, but you know a lot of men like him. His wife, Liz, relinquished her own career to raise their two children. She sustained the family through several moves and more than a few teenage crises.

Soon, the children will be leaving home for college.

Ben and Liz met at graduate school. Afterward, they both made outstanding progress in their careers. He was with a large industrial corporation, she with a major bank.

Liz quit her job after five years to have children. She never went back to paid work although her workweek with her toddlers was even longer than her husband's with his company.

There were hundreds of childcare responsibilities. These started at six AM. (Unless one of the kids woke up in the middle of the night, which happened often). There was the annual school auction. Volunteering to help the sixth-grade teacher. The music lessons. Tutors. And later, after-school sports.

At least once a month, Liz accompanied her husband to dinner with out-of-town executives who were visiting the corporate headquarters of his company.

Many of her women friends maintained their careers. Some of them said things to her that were cruelly insensitive. "When are you going back to work?" was a question she could handle. But when one of her friends asked Liz, "When are you going to get a *real* job?" it was too much.

She loved being a mother and having the luxury of spending so much time with her children. Yes, she had other ideas and plans, but she willingly put them on hold.

One evening in early December, after working another long day, Ben leaves the office late in the evening. Sitting on the commuter train, he reflects on the fact that his two daughters are almost young adults.

He wonders what his wife will do once they leave home.

A close colleague of his has just gone through a bitter divorce. Ben wants to know what went wrong. And could it happen to him?

"What happened?" Ben asks his colleague one night over a glass of wine at a nearby café.

"She was angry at me. Said I never gave her the intimacy she wanted in our marriage. She also resented staying at home while I pursued my career."

Ben is certain his own wife isn't angry like that. But then . . . he isn't completely sure. It isn't a topic they ever discussed.

Ben's colleague is shattered by the painful failure of his marriage. As they leave the café that evening, he tells Ben, "You ought to ask Liz what she'd like to do now that the kids are growing up.

One of the last things my wife told me was, 'You always focused on *your* dreams, but never asked about *mine*.'"

Great artists and leaders stay as close to their dreams as we stray from them. "Dreams are the touchstones of our characters," wrote Thoreau, a man who delighted in his own imagination. Van Gogh told a friend, "I dream my painting, and then I paint my dreams."

On the train home, Ben thinks a great deal about what his colleague has said. He is right—he and Liz never talk about it. He doesn't think about her dreams, let alone his own. He enjoys his work, yet sometimes he wonders if the ladder he is climbing is leaning against the wrong wall.

That night, over a late dinner, Ben looks up at Liz and asks her a simple question:

"What are your dreams, Liz?"

"What?"

"I am wondering . . . what dreams do you have? You used to talk about going back to school, perhaps getting that degree. Do you remember?"

Liz looks down at her plate, and when she looks up again there are tears welling up in her eyes.

"You've never . . . you've never, ever asked me that before," she says. They stay at the table and talk for two hours. She pours out her dreams, her hopes, and her fears. He just listens. It is nearly midnight before they go to bed.

Relationships atrophy when you take them for granted. Don't just go through the motions! Treat your spouse or partner like a newlywed. Treat old clients like brand new ones. Greet a friend as if you haven't seen him in a year. Use this simple question—*what are your dreams?*—to show you care and to help reconnect people to their greatest longings.

Absorbed by the details of our day-to-day lives, we are rarely allowed to dream. Invite a friend or loved one to share their heart with you. Ask: **"What are your dreams?"**

Suggestions for How to Use This Question

"What are your dreams?"

This is a deceptively simple yet powerful question that most of us are afraid to ask, perhaps because we think it would be too intrusive. Maybe we are afraid of what the answer will be. Yet, everyone loves to dream, and we all have dreams.

It can be a magical moment for others when you invite them to share their dreams with you.

When to use the question
- When you want to connect with and get closer to a loved one or friend.
- When you want to help someone reconnect to their passion and their aspirations.

Alternative versions of the question
- "What things would you like to do in your life that you haven't gotten around to yet?"
- "If you had no constraints—children, money, your spouse's job, whatever—what would you like to do?"

Follow-up questions
- "What would be most rewarding about that for you?"
- "What could make that possible?"
- "What's getting in the way of doing that?"

15 | Silence Can Be the Best Answer

"Call me as soon as you possibly can. I need to talk with you."

I am in the receiving line following the 11 o'clock service at our church. That's when Tom Sewell, our minister, grabs my arm and whispers he is desperate to see me. I am Chairman of the Church Board, and Tom and I are very close.

I call him very first thing Monday morning. I don't know what to think. The truth is, I am thinking the worst.

The following day, I'm sitting in Tom's book-lined office. I can see he's going through a high level of torment. I've never seen him quite like this.

"I've been offered a new position," Tom tells me. "You remember I missed services four Sundays ago. Well, I was guest preacher at a New York church. They were looking me over. It's the largest and most visible and prestigious in our denomination. They've called me to be their Senior Minister. That would be the most important pulpit in our entire church."

"I'm proud of you," I tell him, "but not surprised. Our church has tripled in size during your time with us and the congregation

73

loves you. Best of all, you live the values you preach. What have you decided?"

"That's the problem," he says. "I can't decide. Nancy isn't in favor of the move. But she'll go with me whatever I decide. I know the kids won't like it at all. They have close friends and they're at an age when they'll really resist moving.

"Tell me, what do you think I should I do?"

I pause and reflect momentarily about Tom's dilemma. Sometimes, when a choice is intensely personal, when the alternatives pull at your gut, it's best to simply dig deep enough to uncover what the person really wants to do.

I decide to use the plus-minus exercise. You know, a line down the middle of the sheet—the advantages on one side of the page, the disadvantages on the other.

I start asking questions. There are plenty of advantages. The salary, the manse, a congregation four times our size, a full-time business manager, and a ministerial staff of seven.

On the other side of the ledger, the entries are even longer. To begin with, Nancy's feelings about staying. The two oldest children are in high school—Ted plays varsity basketball and Fran is class president. It turns out, also, that Tom doesn't particularly like New York.

The list goes on. He would be spending all his time preaching. He'd lose all of the personal contacts and relationships with his members.

If he moves, he would be the face of the church, but not its soul and spirit. On top of all that, our church is just launching a capital campaign. Tom worries about leaving at this critical time. The list of concerns is very long.

I listen to him for several hours.

At last there is a long silence. A total silence. A Benedictine silence. Finally, I quietly ask, "So Tom, on the basis of all you've said, what do you feel is the right decision for you?"

Tom jumps from his chair and gives me a big bear hug. "You gave me the answer. It's so clear. I'm staying."

Actually, I hadn't given him an answer at all. He found his own solution. Somewhere in the background, I hear the theme from *Rocky*.

That was three years ago. Tom never looked back and I've never known a happier person. The congregation continues to grow, the sermons are more inspiring and motivating than ever, and he is going to officiate at marriages of some of the kids who have gone through his Sunday school. He's one happy, fulfilled guy.

There are times when you don't have to give advice. In fact, in some situations you mustn't. If you allow the person to answer their own question, there can be the clarity of light that author Virginia Woolf saw "as moments of being and illumination, those privileged times when truth is perceived in a flash of intuition."

When the choice is deeply personal, ask: **"What do you feel is the right decision for you?"** Be quiet. Don't fill in the silence. Allow the other person to find the correct solution.

Suggestions for How to Use This Question

"What do you feel is the right decision for you?"

Baltasar Gracián, a Spanish Jesuit who lived in the seventeenth century, was a trusted advisor to kings, queens, and wealthy nobles. In his still-popular book, *The Art of Worldly Wisdom*, he wrote: "When you advise a prince, you should appear to be reminding him of something he had forgotten, rather than the light he was unable to see."

Sometimes, your job is to help others go deeply into their hearts and recognize their own decision rather than push them in a particular direction.

When to use the question
- When the choices are extremely close. (When someone cannot make up their mind about two alternatives, more logical analysis may not help.)
- When the decision is a very personal one that may also affect loved ones. (You cannot quantify the impact of moving to a new city on a child. Only the heart can understand that).

Alternative versions of the question
- "What does your heart tell you?"
- "How will this impact your family (spouse, children, loved ones)?"
- "With each of these choices, what regrets do you think you might have—either way— in two years?"

Follow-up questions
- "What would you say is the deciding factor for you?"
- "What's your next step from here?"

16 | The Greatest Teacher

My client's stock price is languishing. It's treading water, going nowhere, like a sailboat in the doldrums. (That's the area near the Equator where the winds will die for weeks at a time, leaving sailors stranded).

Without a rising stock price, the options owned by the company's senior management are worthless. It's hard to hire new executives. They are, in the worst case, susceptible to a hostile raider. The business could be stripped clean, its assets plundered like war booty in medieval times.

The company hires us to figure out why this is happening and to suggest remedial strategies. They are committed to getting to the bottom of things.

We put our best team of analysts on the case. We even seek the collaboration of a brilliant finance professor at the London Business School.

The diagnosis is clear: Investors in this company's stock expect higher returns than the business generates—at least the way it is managed today. This means its cost of equity is higher than its return on equity. One of the major problems is that there is a retail store business saddled with expensive leases and weak product categories. The customer's average purchase is tiny.

They need strong medicine. And it may be a bitter pill to swallow.

We create a report that is leading edge. It incorporates the latest capital markets theories and analytical models. It has charts and graphs that would rival the battle plans for the invasion of Normandy. 172 pages.

We are proud of the depth, thoroughness, and incisiveness of that interim document. It is incontrovertible. Unequivocal.

Our first meeting to present the preliminary recommendations, however, is little short of a disaster. We should have remembered Helmut Von Moltke's warning, "No battle plan survives contact with the enemy."

We're in a large meeting room at the company headquarters, sitting around a table. I begin my presentation. I barely get started when the executives representing the retail business begin attacking every aspect of our analysis. They defend their turf like grizzled, street-smart junkyard dogs. Anticipating our conclusions, they have even *hired their own economist* to refute the assumptions in our analytical models. We are blindsided.

"Well," the CEO, Trevor, sums up diplomatically, "it looks like we need to do a little more work on this to resolve our differences of opinion."

We leave and the report is heavier going back than going in.

Back at our offices, we lick our wounds. My boss, James Kelly, is silent as we conduct a post mortem on the event. James founded our firm. He is brilliant, as thoughtful a problem-solver as I have ever met. A silent-running, deep brook of experience. We spend the first 20 minutes mostly criticizing the client for being so resistant to our well-researched conclusions. (It's so obvious. Can't they see?)

James, who says nothing so far, looks up at me and asks, "What have you learned?"

We all stare at each other, then look side to side. We avoid James's gaze.

"Well," I volunteer, "we should have spent more time with the retail executives."

"Agreed," says James. "And what else? What did you learn about influencing people?"

"It doesn't just come down to the numbers," I answer. "They have deeply held beliefs about their business. They're emotional about it. We have to work at different levels—rational, emotional—to win them over."

James nods. "And don't forget political. Rational, emotional, political. All three must be considered. And what did you learn about relationship management?"

"We focused way too much on Trevor, the CEO. We didn't realize how much he defers to his executives. There's more than one client here. We undervalued the need to build relationships with the other leaders in the organization."

James nods again. "Good. Oh—last thing. What did you learn about preparing for client presentations?"

I smile sheepishly. James has a maxim. He's repeated it many times to us: *Always preview your conclusions with the client.* Never walk into a room unless every client executive present has been briefed on what you're going to say. Always know where they stand beforehand.

(By the way, that advice applies to just about any meeting with an important constituency. It's the same whether you're meeting with a client or with your own organization's leadership to discuss a major proposal.)

"I know," I admit. "Always review our findings beforehand with everyone. Encourage them to get their fingerprints on it."

Three months later, Trevor retires. A new, young CEO is appointed by the board to take over this troubled company.

Richard Early is a hotshot, a take-no-prisoners executive who had already turned around two other major companies.

I have a very brief meeting with him shortly after he arrives, and I share a copy of our analysis with him. All 172 pages!

A week later, his executive assistant calls me. "Mr. Early asks if you could please prepare an executive summary of your report." I ask her what he's looking for. "He wants something in between the one page of summary conclusions at the front and the 172 pages of analysis." I look at the 172 pages sitting on my desk, and grimace. I roll up my sleeves. I have my work cut out for me.

For days, I struggle to summarize our analysis. I work like crazy. No sleep. I don't want just a summary, I want a statement, a manifesto that is clear and bold and compelling.

I finally reduce 172 pages to five, and send them to the new CEO. They are five hard-hitting pages. They tell a story. It's a convincing, lively tale.

But several weeks pass. I hear nothing. I give up hope of continuing our work with this client.

A month later, Richard Early calls me personally on the phone. That is unusual—the CEO, calling me directly. Usually, you are summoned by one of five executive assistants.

"Thanks for the summary," he says. "Now, I finally understand what you guys are saying. I really hadn't seen it clearly before, based on the huge report you gave me. Now it's apparent. It gives the answers we need. In fact, I circulated your summary to my board. I think it makes a compelling case. Can you come up next week? I've got time on Friday. I want to discuss some possible next steps."

Elated, I run to James's office and tell him the good news. The CEO called *me*! James nods approvingly.

"So, what did you learn from this?" he asks me again. Not a single word of congratulations. All he says is, *What did you learn?*

"You don't communicate with CEOs with 100 slides. They digest information in short, concentrated bites."

"Okay," James says. "What else?" I keep thinking.

"Top executives are not interested in methodology," I add.

"That's right. They want to know if they can trust you. Can you do the job? Are you among the best at what you do? Will you always put their interests first? By the way," he continues, "what would you say you have learned about *trust*?"

"More analysis and expertise doesn't build more trust," I say. "We needed to invest in more face-time with this client. And with Richard Early, as soon as he started."

"Anything else?"

I keep thinking about the 172 pages I was so proud of. And the condensed five pages that sold the CEO on our work.

"Sometimes, less is more?" I'm reminded that Louie Armstrong said that it's not the notes that make the music—it's the space between the notes.

James answers me with a smile that slowly fills his face. I'm not sure which does more to make my day—the call from the new CEO, or James's smile.

It's a lesson I had to learn and one I've never forgotten. I'm thinking that a difficult experience is often the best education, but sometimes the tuition is very high.

Setbacks are great teachers, but so are successes. The great Peter Drucker wrote, "Follow effective action with quiet reflection. From the quiet reflection will come even more effective action."

People often race headlong from one activity to the next, never pausing to reflect. To help someone get the most out of their experiences, ask: **"What did you learn?"**

Suggestions for How to Use This Question

"What did you learn?"

This may surprise you: We often do not learn from our experiences. This has been demonstrated repeatedly in research studies conducted by social scientists. We attribute our successes to our own capabilities and performance, whereas we pin failures on other people or external circumstances beyond our control. Woody Allen said that if you can't find someone to blame, you're not trying hard enough.

The U.S. military is one of the few organizations that systematically tries to learn from experience. The "after-action review" is a staple of all military operations, including training exercises. Commanders are brutally honest.

Remember to ask not just "What did you learn?" but also "What did you learn about . . . ?" Perhaps there is a lesson about motivating people, trust, or organizational politics.

When to use the question
- Any time someone is sharing an experience or event with you.
- After any meeting, interview, or visit.
- When you are mentoring or coaching someone.

Alternative versions of the question
- "What's the most memorable thing you took away from that experience?"
- "What did you learn about . . . ?" (people, trust, human nature, motivation, planning, etc.).

Follow-up questions
- "Do you think that's always true, or is this situation particular?"
- "Can you say more about that?"

17 | Push Open the Flood Gate

I am having lunch with Margaret.

I don't usually take time for this sort of luncheon date. But Margaret has been calling every month for the past year to arrange a time we can get together. She is Vice President of the bank where I have my business account, in charge of the Private Banking Division.

I think: Who knows when I'm going to need some credit? Why not get together? I have never met her.

"Sure. You bet, let's have lunch. It's about time," I tell her when she calls this last time. We meet at a special restaurant of her choosing. She is waiting at the table when I arrive. She stands up. Her handshake is firm and friendly.

Before the waiter comes for the order, Margaret talks about how long she has been at the bank. She tells me about her progression up the ladder to her present position. "I've worked very hard to get where I am."

The waiter arrives with the clam chowder. While we are eating that, I hear about her wonderful two-week holiday in Hawaii.

"We go there every year. We have a time-share on the Big Island. It's glorious."

(I wonder where this is going. There's a wonderful scene in *Scarface*, when Al Pacino is relaxing in a huge bubble bath in his mansion. He looks around and asks, "Is this all there is?" I'm asking the same question.)

Between the soup and our Cobb salad, Margaret tells me about her new grandchild. She digs into her purse and pulls out some photos for me to look at. There's nothing as proud as a new grandmother.

(I am wondering if Margaret has any questions for me. Nothing so far.)

We finish with coffee.

She looks at her watch. As sudden as a sneeze, it's obvious it is time to leave. "It is so special," she says, "having this time with you. I've really looked forward to meeting you."

Whoa—what's happening here? It occurs to me that I learned a great deal about Margaret. She learned nothing about me. Nothing. She has no idea what motivates me or what makes me get up in the morning. She's learned nothing about my business.

Just think about what she could discover with some simple, open-ended questions. For instance, "Tell me how you feel about the bank's services?" Or, "Why did you decide to go into business for yourself?" Or, "You're an important client of ours—how can we do a better job of meeting your needs?"

Most important: "Really? Can you tell me more?"

An amazing torrent of conversation and information flows when someone responds to a question of yours and you say, "Tell me more." This simple phrase, in fact, can be used almost anytime to draw someone out. "Tell me more about that" is a powerful prompt you can use often. Probably daily.

I left the restaurant, shaking my head.

Back at my office, a colleague asks me about my lunch. "Was it a good use of your time?"

"No!" I blurt out, before I could even think of a proper response.

"Why? What happened?" he asks. And as I think about the lunch, I realize my banker did not ask me anything that helps me clarify my thinking about my business or my career. Nor did she share with me, for example, how some of her other clients, in similar businesses, deal with my particular challenges. By failing to learn about my priorities, she gleaned no clue about how to serve me better or what other services I could benefit from.

Dear reader, do we see the same thing? We have to get together and compare notes to make absolutely sure, but I think we do.

My banker squandered a power-packed opportunity. She goes through business life's revolving door on somebody else's push. She could have ensured my continuing relationship with the bank. She could have won my enthusiastic business support wrapped in a perfect package with few strings remaining untied. She didn't.

It's not about you. If you do all the talking, you learn nothing about the person. If you do all the talking you're in the spotlight. If you do all the talking, you don't empower the other person.

Your job is not to listen and respond. Your job is to gain information and create a vibrant dialogue. That's an important distinction. *Tell me more* is the magic key to open up the next layer of the other person's thinking and experiences.

Gain more information and open the other person up by asking, **"Can you tell me more?"** Ask it often. It is to conversations what fresh-baked bread with soft creamery butter is to a meal.

Suggestions for How to Use This Question

"Can you tell me more?

A woman has dinner, within one month, with two great rival British statesmen of the nineteenth century, Gladstone and Disraeli. Both have been Prime Minister of the country. When asked to compare the two men, she says, "After my dinner with Mr. Gladstone, I thought he was the cleverest man in all of England." When her friends ask about her second evening out, she replies, "After my dinner with Mr. Disraeli, I felt as though *I* were the cleverest woman in all of England!"

When you make the conversation all about you, others may think you are clever. But you will not build their trust. You will not learn about them. You will squander an opportunity to build the foundations for a rich, long-term relationship.

When to use the question
- Often and everywhere.
- As a general prompt to encourage someone to go deeper and say more.

Alternative versions of the question
- "Can you say more about that?"
- "What do you mean by . . . ?" (ask them to define their terms more carefully)

Follow-up questions
- "When . . . ?"
- "What . . . ?"
- "How . . . ?
- "Why . . . ?

18 | The Essence of Your Job

I'm at lunch with my client, Claire. She runs a division of a large, public company. We arrive early, and the restaurant is nearly empty.

Claire and I meet two or three times a year, usually to debrief on the advisory work I'm doing for Claire's organization. Our conversation begins with small talk. Then it shifts to a discussion about the initiatives I am helping to develop for her division.

By the time we are finishing the main course, we have exhausted the marketing discussion. This almost always happens. After all, who wants to talk about business for an entire meal?

The patrons are lined up at the door now, and the restaurant is nearly full.

Activist Ralph Nader once said, "I don't think meals have any business being deductible. I'm for separation of calories and corporations." I disagree. Meals are good for relationship building. Research shows that we feel more favorably toward someone if we share a meal. Meals can have an important business purpose.

There is silence as the waiter clears our plates. I look up at Claire. I decide to shift the conversation. "How are *you* doing?" I ask.

"Good, I'm good." More silence. "It's been pretty relentless."

"Relentless?" (Sometimes, just echoing the last word of someone's sentence will cause more to be revealed.)

"There are my external commitments. You know, seeing key customers, meeting with suppliers, and so on. Then, all the day-to-day internal management I am involved in. It's a 70-hour week that could become 100 if I let it." She heaves a sigh.

I want to ask about the details of her work, to dissect her effectiveness with each constituency. The problem-solver in me is chomping at the bit.

Instead, I take a breath and pause.

"Claire, I'm curious . . . you've been in the divisional CEO role now for over a year. As you think about the job, what things do you wish you could spend *more* time on, and what activities do you wish you could do *less* of?"

She reflects for a minute. I can see her brain is suddenly churning.

"Hmm . . . that's an interesting question." Another pause.

"First of all, I wish I had more time to spend on coaching and mentoring the executives on my leadership team. I love doing it, and I'm good at it. And I know they can be much better than they are today. Second, we've got an ambitious strategy to develop lower-cost products for emerging markets. Yet, I've never even been to many of the countries we want to sell to."

An hour later we are still sitting at the lunch table. The line at the maitre d's station is gone. The tables are mostly empty again.

I've learned more about Claire's priorities than I thought possible. I know what frustrates her. I understand how she would like to refocus her time going forward.

A few months later, Claire completely reorganizes her office and creates a new position to provide additional support for her. When I see her next, I smell a new zest for her role, an enthusiasm that I haven't seen since she was promoted.

I wanted to dissect the individual pieces of Claire's role and suggest small improvements. That requires *analysis*. It's when you pull something apart and assess the components one by one. "Improve your meeting management!" Or, "Delegate more effectively!" It would have helped, but only a little.

What Claire really needed was a completely fresh look at her role and her priorities. That requires *synthesis*. You look at the whole first. You also look at personal strengths and preferences. For that, I needed to ask a question that would push her to sit back and reflect on the totality of her job.

To get someone to reflect on their job (or their life), ask: **"What parts of your job do you wish you could spend more time on, and what things do you wish you could do less of?"**

Suggestions for How to Use This Question

"What parts of your job do you wish you could spend more time on, and what things do you wish you could do less of?"

Many factors influence how we spend our time: Historic accident, other peoples' demands, and our tendency to follow the path of least resistance. By stepping back, we can often finally see the forest and not just the trees.

This question is a wonderful way to get people talking about their job—whether it's running a company or running a household. You'll lead them down a path of reflection that may result in joyous and transformative changes.

When to use the question
- To invite another person to talk about their position and their role in an organization.
- In particular, around the time of someone's anniversary in a job—one year, three years, and so on.
- To explore a friend, colleague, or family member's life and help them understand how they might refocus their time.

Alternative versions of the question
- "Which are the most enjoyable parts of your job, and which parts do you find least enjoyable?"
- "If you had an extra couple of hours in each week, how would you spend them?"
- "What do you wish you could devote more time to?"

Follow-up questions
- "What's getting in the way of making that change?"
- "I know it's difficult to drop or spend less time on some of those things you mentioned . . . but what might possibly enable you to do that?"

19 | A Tempest-Tossed Topic

The waiter brings three steaming entrees to our dinner table. Then a moment later, two more.

I'm having dinner with Chuck Colson and his wife, Patty. We're at our favorite Chinese restaurant. Chuck is my hero.

I thought I knew just about every detail in his life—virtually every bit of information. At dinner, I uncovered something more. That's because I asked a question I had never raised with him before.

In a moment, I'll tell you about the question I asked. It's truly a power question. When I ask it, we talk for two full hours—from Moo Shu pork to fortune cookies.

But first, let me tell you about Charles W. Colson. I'll give you only a peek into this extraordinary man's life. His autobiography, *Born Again*, sold over 3 million copies. (The royalties for this bestseller went entirely to the founding of Prison Fellowship. In fact, the royalties for all his many books are given to this ministry.)

You may remember him going to jail because of his involvement in the Watergate scandal and the conspiracy. (He actually never did take part in this—but that's another story.)

Still in his thirties, Chuck became Special Counsel to President Nixon. His office was right next to the hideaway office of the President. Nixon hated the Oval Office and spent most of his time in his secluded sanctuary.

Chuck was part of Nixon's unofficial Cabinet. He was included in major policy issues. It would not be unusual for Colson to be called at two in the morning for a chat or to be summoned into Nixon's office regularly during the day.

But I knew all that. And, of course, I knew about his going to prison because of trumped-up evidence about his involvement in the conspiracy.

A question I had never asked Chuck before, that I often ask others, was: "What was the most difficult question you have ever been asked?

I wasn't at all prepared for Chuck's response. I thought it would have something to do with his founding of Prison Fellowship.

Colson says that going to prison was the most significant thing that ever happened to him. The *New York Times* wrote, "Colson's life displayed the most extraordinary redemption in history."

His three-year sentence was committed to seven months. But in that time, the seeds were planted for Prison Fellowship. He says it's not what happens to you in life that matters. It's how you handle it that determines your character.

Prison Fellowship grew to become the largest organization in the world for the rehabilitation of prisoners. It operates in 110 countries. A large percentage of its graduates stay out of prison after their release, unlike the vast majority of other prisoners who are soon back behind bars. Colson is the father of a movement that has now spawned hundreds of similar organizations.

Back to my question: "What is the most difficult question you have ever been asked?" It turns out it has nothing to do with his time in prison, nor all his years as the world's greatest reformer of prisoners. I'll let him tell the story as he told it to me.

"President Nixon calls me into his office. It's late at night. We're sitting alone.

"I can tell you, we're all feeling pretty ecstatic. His second term victory was at the time the largest landslide in the history of the country. He could do no wrong." (It's before Watergate.)

"He explains to me he just received a cable from Henry Kissinger (Secretary of State). Kissinger strongly suggests that at the same time we are suing for peace in Vietnam, we should increase the bombing of North Vietnam. This seems to him to be not only reasonable, but essential if we are to be taken seriously by the North at the peace table.

But Kissinger tells Nixon something else. He says it is important that the President explain to the American people why this is essential. That Nixon open it up to public discussion and debate.

"'Chuck,' Nixon says, 'I'm not at all sure about this. I need to know what you think. I trust your judgment. Should we carry on the bombing and go back to the public to explain our policy?'

"It is a very tough call," Chuck continues. "Kissinger is brilliant, and he carries great clout with the President. But ultimately, I think he is wrong on this one.

"It is also a difficult question because of the public outrage over the lack of transparency around the war. Nixon has to balance the need to create public debate and support against doing everything possible to force a peace agreement.

"We talk a good bit more. It's a minefield, this question. But I finally tell the President what I think: We should continue the bombing, but not try to explain it. I am afraid it will lead to more bitter debate in the country and contentious demonstrations. Everyone is sick about Vietnam and the war. Most important, trying to explain it will undermine our chances for success at the peace negotiations.

"That is the toughest question I've ever been asked. It is a harrowing, complex issue. And you don't go up against the Secretary of State lightly.

"We do, by the way, sustain the bombing, which did in fact help speed the peace negotiations."

Reader, would you like to know more about the conspiracy, John Dean, Ehrlichman, Haldeman, John Mitchell, and that whole bunch? Well . . . that's another story for another time.

We often learn the most when we experience intense pressure—when we are stretched and pushed. Learn from the deepest recesses of someone's experience by asking, **"What is the most difficult question you have ever been asked?"**

Suggestions for How to Use This Question

"What was the most difficult question you have ever been asked?

Elie Wiesel wrote that God created the Earth and made humans because God loves stories, and all of our lives are the stories He tells.

What is the most difficult question you have ever been asked almost always creates a flowing stream of conversation. When asked the question, what you will most often find is that the person stops and says, "Okay—what's going on here? Let me think. Wow! That's a tough one. In my heart of hearts, what is the answer?"

When to Use This Question
- When you want to plumb deep into the person's psyche.
- When you want to know much more about the character and makeup of the person.

Alternate versions of the question
- "What is the most profound question you have ever been asked? That *you* have ever asked anyone?"
- "Tell me, have you ever been asked a question that really stumped you?"
- "Have you ever been asked a question that embarrassed you, or have you ever asked a question that turned out to be embarrassing for the person you're talking with?"

Follow-up questions
- "What kind of an impact did the question make on your life?"
- "Sometime later, did you feel you gave the right answer?"
- "If you were asked the same question today, would your answer be the same?"

20 | The Road Taken

It all begins with the black bag—my father's black physician's bag.

It's the kind that doctors rarely use today but were popular in the 1950s. It is large and rectangular, with rounded corners, made of pebbled, matte black leather. Inside are all sorts of mysterious packets and vials. Syringes, even. It is full of cures that my father can pull out and use to fix people at will. That black bag is alluring, powerful, magical. At age six I resolve that I, too, will become a doctor.

Most of my family was in medicine. My father's father had also been a doctor, a successful urologist. My mother had been a World War II nurse. My oldest brother entered medical school when I was a senior in high school.

In college I became pre-med. That means I had to sign up for calculus, biology, and a raft of other science courses. For me, however, it was always going to be a tough row to hoe. Getting into medical school—then as now—was a very difficult challenge. You had to spend your four years of college in the library. You needed top grades. (Getting good grades wasn't the problem. It was getting them consistently in math and science!)

I didn't really care for those pre-med requirements. I found them dry. They didn't grab my heart. Instead, I thrived in the courses I took on literature, history, and languages.

But I gritted my teeth and dug in—those science courses were simply an obstacle I had to jump over to get to my goal. After all, I had always wanted to be a doctor. Everyone in my family had been or was going to be in medicine. During my freshman year my other brother informed us that he, too, was going to apply to medical school.

The pressure grew. Come hell or high water, I too would one day have a black, pebbled-leather doctor's bag!

During my sophomore year I see an ad in the college newspaper: "Career Guidance Seminar. *Learn to write an effective resume.*"

I think, Why not? Perhaps it will help me get a good summer job. Having attractive summer positions on my record will enhance my medical school applications.

I don't realize it, but I'm arriving at a turning point. I mean one of those really big forks in the road, the kind that happen only a few times in your life. It's when you choose a spouse. Decide on a career. Debate whether or not to accept a promotion and move halfway around the world.

In his poem "The Road Not Taken," Robert Frost elegantly describes what it feels like to face such a turning point. It's a beloved poem. He describes coming to a fork in the road while strolling in a yellow wood. He says that both roads have about equal quantities of leaves on them, although one seems a bit less traveled. He has a dilemma: Which fork should he take? Which choice is the right one?

Frost ends the poem with these lines:

> Two roads diverged in a wood, and I—
>   I took the one less traveled by,
>   And that has made all the difference.

The poem is about how *difficult* it is to make life-changing decisions. It's about how close the choices seem to be to each other.

And how, afterward, we want to believe our choice was the right one for us.

At these forks, we must decide and commit!

I sign up for the career development workshop. For two days, we learn how to write a resume. How to best highlight our prior experience and education. We study interviewing techniques. How to network.

On the second afternoon, we are given the final assignment. "This is your last exercise," the instructor tells us.

"Take a sheet of paper. During the next hour, you are to write your obituary. You are to write the article about your life that will appear in the local newspapers after you die. How would you like it to read? What kind of a life will it describe? Now, get started."

Some of us gasp. Our obituary? When you're 20 years old, you are immortal. You are never going to die. Why this morbid exercise?

I begin writing. I describe an illustrious medical career. In my obituary, I have been a prominent physician who held a professor-ship at a major medical school (just like my father). I had also had a large clinical practice (just like my father). And more. I imagine how proud my parents will have been. The steady income. The accolades.

But after 20 minutes, I abruptly stop in mid-sentence. I feel a slight panic. My heart is racing.

What am I writing? I put my pen down. I am thunderstruck.

What I really want to do is travel. To live abroad. To be an entrepreneur.

The prospect of years of medical training suddenly seems over-whelming. Four years of taking courses that hold only moderate interest for me. Four years of living in perpetual anxiety about get-ting into medical school. Then four years of medical school itself. Afterwards, a residency of three to five years. Later, perhaps a post-graduate fellowship.

I don't really want to study organic chemistry. I suddenly realize I'm studying it for my father. For my grandfather. But not for me.

No, I want to learn foreign languages and study great novels. A voice in me is shouting, "Are you really sure you want to become a doctor! You're becoming a doctor for *them*, not for you! What about all that traveling you want to do?"

A giddy resolve comes over me.

I cross out the first page, about becoming a prominent and respected physician. I pause, and then start to write again. But this time, it's a different story. A different future.

In my new obituary I have a career in international business. I am fluent in four languages. I run businesses in Europe. I even write a couple of business books. I travel the world. Teach some courses at a business school. I sketch a radically different career trajectory. I also write about my marriage and three children. And many interesting friends.

I'm only 20 years old. I'm writing my obituary. What I'm really writing is my life's plan. A plan that excites me. My plan. Not my father's.

Years later, I misplaced that piece of paper. But I never forgot what I wrote on it.

The morning after the workshop is Sunday. I walk to the end of the hallway in my dormitory. Put a dime in the pay phone. As usual, it's a collect call—my weekly call to my father and mother.

"Dad, I have decided not to go to medical school."

I wait for the disapproval, the lecturing tone, the advice intended to buck me up. It never comes.

"I don't care whether or not you go to medical school. I am happy for you to pursue whatever career you'd like."

(I'm thinking: *Did he say that? No! It's not possible!*)

"Really?"

"Really. No one in the family feels you have to become a doctor."

I am shocked. Flabbergasted. The telephone receiver is sliding out of my hand. I exhale slowly, grinning from ear to ear. I want to hug my father.

You're probably wondering, "How did things turn out? What happened?" I will tell you: Things turned out well. And virtually all of it happened just as I wrote it in my obituary, at age 20.

To help someone reflect on what they'd truly like to do in their lives, and how they'd like to be remembered by others, ask: **"If you had to write your obituary today, what would you like it to say about you and your life?"**

Suggestions for How to Use This Question

"If you had to write your obituary today, what would you like it to say about you and your life?"

Obituaries are normally for those who stay behind. They help the family and friends of those who have departed celebrate their lives.

An obituary can become something important to the living in another way. Envisioning it ahead of time can help shape your life. It can bring what's most important to you—and what you truly enjoy—into sharp focus. Writing your obituary now will highlight the choices you are making and can make.

When to use this question
- When coaching or mentoring someone.
- When a young person is making important career and life choices.

Alternative versions of the question
- "Looking ahead in your life, what do you think will give you the greatest sense of achievement? The most personal fulfillment?"
- "What are some things you haven't done but which you would like to do before you die?"

Follow-up questions
- "Why did you put those particular things in your obituary?"
- "What could get in the way of accomplishing that?"

21 | Who Do *You* Say I Am?

A financial executive leaves his office tower on Wall Street, walks past City Hall, goes east on Worth Street, and onto the Bowery. Empty bottles and garbage litter the door stoops. People are sleeping in cardboard boxes. In front of a shelter, he meets a homeless woman—a woman with a tortured life history. She is clutching a paper cup of black coffee. She looks at his crisp navy suit and wonders, *What is he doing here*?

He turns to her and quietly asks, "Could you get me a cup?" That simple question leads to an extraordinary conversation, and a changed life.

A real event? *Re-imagined* would be the best description. This encounter did actually take place, although it was long ago and far away from New York City.

Two thousand years ago, a Jewish Rabbi named Jesus walks through the desert with his 12 disciples. He is traversing Samaria, a region into which Jesus's Israelite contemporaries would not venture. Sitting next to an isolated well in the desert, outside of a small town, Jesus waits until a lone woman appears.

"Will you give me a drink?" he asks. It's actually a shocking question. Jews of that day will never, not ever, associate with Samaritans. They are considered detestable and unclean. The woman is taken aback. She responds, "How can you ask me for a drink? For Jews do not talk to Samaritans." He draws her out, and uncovers a troubled past. She has had many husbands, many men in her life. She is an outcast even in her own village.

Their subsequent conversation, about how Jesus can help the woman's spiritual emptiness and social isolation, has been studied for centuries. The encounter, which Jesus starts with the question, "Will you give me a drink?" transforms her.

Jesus was a revolutionary. He wanted nothing less than to overturn the established order and save humankind from its own brokenness. In His kingdom, esteem for power, money, and status would be replaced by humility, service, and love for one's neighbor.

Asking *questions* was one of His main tools for transforming others.

At times, Jesus would ask a simple question to reach out to a marginalized person. A person who did not expect to be treated with respect—let alone spoken to—by a man and a member of the educated class. He spoke to prostitutes, lepers, beggars, criminals, and the downcast.

He used "counter-questions" to fend off the religious authorities of the day. They would ask Him a question intended to trick Him into incriminating Himself. Instead of answering, He would counter their questions with a question of His own. A question He knew they could not adequately answer. He asked deep, rhetorical questions, to make His followers and the people He encountered think.

Jesus asked His most penetrating and profound question just before His final entry into Jerusalem.

He gathers His disciples around him in the region of Caesarea Philippi. He asks them, "Who do people say the Son of Man is?"

"Well," they reply, "Some say John the Baptist. Others say Elijah. Then there are those who say Jeremiah or one of the other prophets." There is a thundering silence. Jesus gives a piercing look into the eyes of each disciple. Then, the most direct question ever asked. He turns to Simon Peter:

"But who do *you* say I am?" Jesus needs to know. Peter stands up. It becomes very quiet. He looks at Jesus.

"You are the Messiah, the Son of the living God."

Within a week, Jesus will be accused, tried, and crucified. His disciples will be bereft of their leader.

Why does Jesus ask *this* question at this critical juncture in His short ministry—"Who do you say I am?" Why not, "Do you think you can manage on your own now?" or "Would you like a few more tips from me before I perish next week?"

Think about it this way: He knows He is going to die on the cross, and has repeatedly told his followers that this will be His fate.

He wants His revolution, His kingdom of heaven, to take root and grow after He is gone from the physical world. But He needs to know if they truly understand who He is and what He stands for. He wants to hear a personal proclamation of faith.

If He is just another wise Rabbi, then they can all go back to their day jobs—fishing, tax collecting, doctoring. They can forget about the three years they have spent with Jesus.

But if they truly believe He is the Messiah, they will be un-equivocally and completely committed to His values of humility, servant leadership, and building a direct relationship with God through Him. Yes, if they believe, He knows they will have the energy and inspiration to carry on. It takes the resurrection appear-ances of Jesus, after his crucifixion, to cement their faith. And they do carry on—even though it costs most of them their lives.

Are you a leader in an organization? A business professional? A parent? A teacher? In any of these roles, you need to know if those around you understand who you are. You need to know if they truly appreciate the beliefs and values that define you. They need to know what you stand for—and what you don't stand for.

Do others know who you really are?

Do those around you understand what you stand for? Ask them this direct question: **"How do you see me as a leader?"** (. . . **or, as a colleague, friend, parent?**)

Suggestions for How to Use This Question

"How do you see me as a leader?" (. . . or, as a colleague, friend, parent?)

We take for granted that the people who work for us or with us understand and respect what we stand for—that they appreciate our values and approach to work. The same goes in our personal lives, with regard to our family members and friends. But do they know who we really are? How do we know?

You can create a truly intimate and inspired conversation by asking this question. You may learn something unexpected.

When to use the question
- Any time you want to know how others perceive your leadership.
- To discover if those closest to you—family, friends, colleagues—understand who you are and what you stand for.
- To shake people up who are on the fence about your intentions.

Alternative versions of the question
- "What do *you* think I stand for?"
- "If you were to summarize the principles or values I exemplify, what would some of them be?"

Follow-up questions
- "What have I done that has really reinforced that?"
- "What else could I do to better communicate and be a role model for these things?"
- "Why do you think that?"

22 | That Special Moment in Life

Get ready. I'm going to ask you the power question that this chapter is all about.

What was the happiest day of your life?

Was it the day you got that all-important promotion? When your first child was born? The day you met your future spouse? Or perhaps when you married?

What day was special for you beyond all others? What memory, even years later, still makes you smile?

Take a minute and think about this question. What was the happiest day of your life, your best moment? Get your answer firmly in your mind. Savor it. When you finish, read on. I am going to share with you a story about Bob.

You've met a few people in your life like him. But not many. They walk into a room and they command the space. Their very presence fills the room.

That's Bob. He's one of those people.

I'm talking about Robert Reynolds, Chief Executive Officer and President of Putnam Investments. It's one of the five top investment houses in the country.

When he went to Putnam, the company was in shambles. There were a number of years of bad returns and civil charges involving improper trading. You wonder why Bob, the darling of the financial world at the time, would want to take on that kind of challenge.

Well, he has turned it around. The *Wall Street Journal* wrote about him launching a whole new era at Putnam. The paper goes on to say, "He has restored the company's reputation as well as performance."

"When I first arrived at Putnam," Bob says to me, "I found a staff focused on not losing more money. I told them if they wanted to stick around, they had better focus instead on *making* money."

His office is a cornucopia of photographs, statues, mementos, and gifts he received when he left Fidelity, the big gorilla in the investment business. I'll tell you more about his involvement there in a moment.

First let me tell you about this visit with Bob. I ask him lots of questions. I do this on every visit when I meet with someone. There's one question that usually elicits a poignant response (and is the most inner-reaching): *What is the greatest disappointment in your life?*

I ask Bob this question. I don't get a glimmer from him.

I figure I know the answer. I'm thinking it's too bitter a memory for him to talk about. But Bob finally responds.

"You know, I don't really experience disappointments. I can't really remember any major ones. I'm a very positive guy."

I probe a bit more. I think I know Bob fairly well. I am pretty certain he will tell me the great disappointment in his life is not getting the job as Commissioner of the National Football League. He had actually been told he was the choice of the team owners.

"There were a number of candidates. Then it got down to eight. Then four. Then finally an internal candidate and me.

"I get a call from Paul Tagliabue. He was Commissioner at the time and just retiring. He says to me, 'I think you're the guy, Bob. We should talk.' I went to see him and had a good meeting.

"And no, in the end I wasn't offered the job. But I actually wasn't disappointed. I was proud I was even a candidate and got as far as I did."

I cover a great deal of ground with Bob on this three-hour visit. There is a lot of catching up to do.

I decide to ask him another power question. "Think back, Bob. What has been the happiest day in your life? The very happiest."

"That's easy. It was the day Ned Johnson (the founder of Fidelity Investments) tells me I would be his successor, the Chief Executive Officer. I am absolutely thrilled. It is the culmination of so much.

"As it turns out, it doesn't end up that way. If you want the details, check *Fortune* magazine. It's a long story. But it was an amiable parting. It was just time to leave."

When he left Fidelity, Bob was number two at the company and Chief Operating Officer.

We talked a long time about Fidelity. As well as I know Bob, I had never explored this with him. "*What has been the happiest day in your life?*"

That's what opened up a great deal of insight into his Fidelity experience. It's very hard and at times stressful to be number two in a family business—especially if there are members of the family on the staff you're supervising. Akin to that, I'm reminded of a similar story.

Someone asked Christian Herter what it was like being the second in command under John Foster Dulles, Secretary of State. "It's very hard being number two in a one-person department."

In my session with Bob, the question that produced the most substantial response is, "*What has been the happiest day in your life?*" Every time I ask someone this question, the reaction is deeply revealing.

Keep in mind that what might be the happiest day for one person may not necessarily be the most joyful for another.

President John Adams wrote in his journal one day: "I went fishing with Charles. It was the worst day in my life." His son, nine-year-old Charles, wrote in his journal. "I went fishing today with father. It was the happiest day in my life."

Dig deep and learn something special about the other person. You will also bring a smile to their face when you ask, **"What has been the happiest day of your life?"**

Suggestions for How to Use This Question

"What has been the happiest day of your life?"

This question can illuminate a darkened room and brighten someone's black mood. The other person may not even be able to answer it—or provide a single answer. That's okay! You will set their mind in motion, flipping through the most pungent memories in their life.

Whether the answer is a revelation or just thoughtful silence, this question always has a positive if not thrilling impact.

When to use the question
- Any time you want to deepen your understanding of the other person and build a stronger relationship with them.
- To understand the important events that have shaped someone's character.

Alternative versions of the question
- "What was the greatest day of your life?"
- "What event in your life has brought you the greatest joy?"

Follow-up questions
- "Why was that so special for you?"
- "Are there any other days or events that stand out for you?"

23 | Your Plans or Their Plans?

Gathered in the boardroom are the eight most senior executives of one of the largest financial institutions in the world. Individual bottles of both sparkling and flat mineral water are carefully arranged around the zebrawood conference table. The only sound is a slight whirr as a discrete white projection screen slides down from a hidden recess in the ceiling.

"You can tell them to come in now," one of the eight tells an attendant.

The management consultants enter and shake hands all around. These consultants represent one of the most prestigious, blue-chip management consulting firms in the world. It is an organization that wields such behind-the-scenes influence that a leading business publication dubbed its partners the "Jesuits of the modern business world." A book on the consulting industry calls them the "lords of strategy."

Today, they are one of three finalists competing to win a major project for the bank's CEO and his team. It's a very large contract.

This is one of the most coveted assignments in the entire management consulting industry. The stakes could not be higher.

The presentation lasts an hour. An occasional polite question is thrown across the burnished table. The lead partner of the consulting firm, Westervelt, goes in depth into corporate banking, one of the bank's main business lines. He chooses the subject to demonstrate how the firm would think about developing a new strategy for the bank. He is brilliant.

(He must have been familiar with my father's maxim, "There is no substitute for genuine lack of preparation." Westervelt is nothing if not fully and utterly prepared).

He knows the large corporate market inside out and is familiar with all the bank's key competitors. He displays a verbal fluency that is mesmerizing. No "ums" or "you knows" from this master of elocution.

Westervelt's presentation is a *tour de force*. Surely he is one of the world's leading experts in this sector. Probably there is no other consultant, anywhere, who could trump his extraordinary knowledge and experience.

Only a few minutes of their time allocation remain. Westervelt pauses. "Are there any other questions?" Heads shake from side to side around the room.

"Thank you very much," says the CEO. "That was very instructive."

As they ride the elevator down from the forty-seventh floor, one of the younger partners says to Westervelt, "You were awesome."

Westervelt smiles. He and his partners feel good about the presentation. Why shouldn't they? They know banking inside and out.

Back in the conference room, the bank executives huddle for a quick debriefing. The consultants they have heard are the CEO's favorites. I know, because the CEO had told me they were. He wants them to get the job. But he isn't going to impose them on his team. There are many positive comments as he goes around the table. Good so far.

The most restrained comes from Jennifer, the bank's chief human resources officer. She has worked with the bank for nearly 30 years. The last to speak is Peter, the head of global corporate banking—the very business the consultants had spent the most time on.

Peter is clearly upset after the consultants' presentation. He is slightly red in the face. Agitated.

"I couldn't possibly have these people as my consultants," he blurts out. He can hardly contain his anger. "Especially the lead partner, Westervelt. He doesn't listen. *He . . . he has no empathy!*"

Concerned, the CEO asks him to elaborate.

"They asked us almost no questions about our strategy and our plans. About the choices we've made. About the strengths we can bring to bear in trying to grow the business. They did not acknowledge our own leading position in corporate banking. They were just full of themselves. Especially Westervelt."

Later on, the CEO also hears from Jennifer, his Human Resources head, who sat through the consultants' presentation. "He never made eye contact with me," she tells the CEO in private. "Not once. It was like I wasn't in the room. They focused the presentation entirely on you. It makes you wonder. What would it be like working with them day-to-day? I don't think their style is aligned with our culture."

A few days later, the CEO calls the consultants to tell them they have lost the job. It's not that they didn't win it. They lost it!

The CEO says something about all the firms being "very close" in their capabilities. Westervelt and his colleagues are surprised. Deeply disappointed. No, crestfallen. How could this happen?

It's one year later. The firm that won the project is still working with the bank. They are now onto their third assignment.

I'm having coffee with the CEO. "I'm curious," I ask him. "In the end, could Westervelt's firm really have done anything different in your bidding process, something that would have made a difference?"

The CEO looks at me. He raises an eyebrow and cocks his head to one side. "Done anything? It was all about one question Westervelt never asked. One simple question he could have asked Peter, about corporate banking: 'Can you tell me about your plans?' He asked *me*. But he never asked Peter himself.

"He overlooked the simplest but most endearing and informative question: *Can you tell me about your plans?*"

A few years ago, I experienced what Peter might have felt in that boardroom. I was going to London on a business trip and planned to spend a few extra days on my own. I met an acquaintance just before leaving. As soon as the word "London" left my lips, he straightened up and cleared his throat. "Oh, you must— you simply *must* stay at the Lanesborough Hotel. Everything else is second rate compared to the Lanesborough. It's your only real choice." There was a heavy silence.

Had my friend bothered to ask about *my* plans, he would have learned I was leaving the next day. He would have discovered I was already booked into a lovely hotel—my favorite—that cost a lot less than the $1,000-a-night Lanesborough.

He didn't ask what my plans were—he told me what they should be. And as a result he came across as an unpleasant and insensitive cad.

Don't start by talking about your own plans. And don't start by talking about your plans for the other person. First, ask them, **"Can you tell me about *your* plans?"**

Suggestions for How to Use This Question

"Can you tell me about your plans?"

To be a great listener, follow these three principles:

Humility. The Indian spiritual leader Mahatma Gandhi said, "To discover the truth, one must become as humble as the dust." You must believe you can learn from every person you encounter.

Curiosity. As we grow older, our curiosity dies. The average five-year-old asks 200 questions a day. How many do you ask? Approach every situation with an intense sense of curiosity, and you will listen more.

Self-awareness. Your biases and prejudices will prevent you from listening to others. Women often make the decision about which new car to buy—yet, in a typical car dealership, the salespeople pay far more attention to the husband. Know yourself!

When to use the question
- Before you tell someone what *you* think their plans should be.
- When you need to understand the other person's intentions and priorities.

Alternate versions of the question
- "How do you plan to approach this?"
- "What is your strategy?"
- "What are your ideas for where you want to go in the future?"

Follow-up questions
- "What process did you use to arrive at that?"
- "What things have you decided *not* to do?"

24 | Never Look Back Unless You Plan to Live That Way

"I feel like I'm being torn apart. I tell you, my heart is breaking. I never felt as bad about anything in my life."

I'm talking with John Kirkman. We're in his office. He's near tears.

John is the owner and manager of a small manufacturing company. He employs about 80 men and women in good times, fewer when things get slow.

"John, I've never before seen you in this state. What the devil is going on?" I'm with John every four or six weeks. We work on his business planning and review his firm's objectives and financial performance.

John tells me he discovered that his Chief Financial Officer was depositing the firm's checks to his own personal account. He finally became aware of the theft. But there is a problem beyond even the $100,000 that was stolen.

He tells me his Chief Financial Officer has been a senior member of the staff for 16 years. On top of that, he is one of John's closest friends and confidants. "I would have trusted him with my life," John tells me.

He says that when he finally confronted Bob (not his real name), John started asking questions.

"Bob, tell me about the money that's missing." Bob goes into a long, unconvincing harangue. He lets John know he is totally innocent. John doesn't buy it.

(There's an expression in Mexico, "con las manos en la masa." It means "with your hands in the bread dough." The English version: caught red-handed. In this case, Bob really did have his hands in the dough).

"I assure you I haven't been taking any money," Bob says. "I wouldn't do that to the firm, and I certainly wouldn't steal from a close friend like you, John."

Bob talks about his family and his time with the firm. He goes on and on. Getting an answer from him is just about as easy as staging a full ballet in a telephone booth.

"His body language tells me everything. His eyes are as dull and lifeless as oysters. His hands are rolled into tight fists. He keeps crossing and uncrossing his legs.

"He admits nothing," John tells me. "He claims he doesn't know anything about the missing money.

"It finally occurs to me that I had been asking a lot of vague, weasel, open-ended questions. And getting weasel answers in response. What I need now is a direct answer—yes or no."

(At times, the value of a closed-ended question is that it can lead to a prized discovery. When asked properly, at precisely the right time, closed-ended questions can be a powerful and crucial ally. You're asking for a direct response. No qualifying. No excuses. No waffling. No babbling.)

John goes on with his story. "Bob, I want a yes or no. No baloney." (John used a stronger word.) "Did you steal the money? Yes or no?"

"I pause," John tells me. "I wait for a response." (The moment is flooded with a crashing silence. I'm thinking that at times, silence is often the very best answer.)

"Several minutes go by. I wait. I don't say a word. Bob finally breaks down. He confesses.

"I'm not certain I would ever have gotten an honest answer if I had continued asking fuzzy, kid-glove questions.

"I am thunderstruck. The theft is such an unexpected, errant act. An aberration after decades of friendship and trust in him.

"Here's my question," John says to me. "He confesses and the darn truth is, I don't know what to do. Should I report him to the authorities? Give him 24 hours to resign? Summarily fire him on the spot, ask for the keys to his office and desk, and escort him out of the building?

"I'm also thinking about Bob's personal situation. One kid still in college. His wife doesn't work. This will for sure destroy him. It's all weighing on me."

Reader, wait! Before you go on, think about what action you would take. Remember, Bob is one of John's closest friends. He is also a first-rate financial officer. Your initial reaction may be to call the police and get Bob as far away from the premises as possible. That's natural. It's a serious crime committed by someone you put great trust in.

I'm going to tell you what happens. I'll also tell you the question I ask John.

"If the circumstances were turned around, John—how would you like to be treated?"

This is a thought-provoking question because it forces a person to forget all of the anger, overlook the disappointment, and put themselves in the other person's shoes. It's a great question because it compels the person to think about how they would like to be dealt with.

Back to my question. "John, how would you like to be treated if the situation was turned around?"

"Hmm. Well, I hadn't thought about it that way. That kind of puts me on the spot. I was so upset, all I could think about was my disappointment.

"I guess I would ask for forgiveness. I would ask for another chance. I would promise that it would never, ever happen again. I would commit to do anything at all to make this horrible thing go away."

"Maybe that's an answer you should consider, John," I suggest. "It may take you a long time to forget—but I do recommend you put that option on the table. After all, didn't you say that's how you would like to be treated?"

Three weeks later I call John. "Tell me what happened with Bob," I ask.

"I forgave him. And I gave him another chance. It was an extraordinary moment. We both cried.

"I tell him in no uncertain terms that we want the money repaid. I give him 120 days. I assure him I will not say anything to anyone in the company or to his wife. Not even my wife. I tell him that what has happened is a closed bond between the two of us. I feel it was the right thing to do. I hope so."

All of this happened years ago. After the incident, John says that Bob worked even harder than before—10- and 12-hour days. He was more dedicated than ever. And he was never dishonest again. Not ever.

Bob is now approaching his twenty-fifth anniversary with the firm. He continues to be one of John's closest friends and is doggedly loyal. He is one of John's most beloved and trusted business confidants.

Sometimes, the right solution to a dilemma you have with someone will present itself when you contemplate a reversal of the roles.

It's a question you can't run away from. "If the circumstances were turned around, how would you like to be treated?"

When you are asked for your advice about a dilemma, explore all options by asking: **If the circumstances were turned around, how would you like to be treated ?**

Suggestions for How to Use This Question

"If the circumstances were turned around, how would you like to be treated?"

Everyone loves the adage, "Do unto others as you would have others do unto you." It's warm and fuzzy. It makes perfect sense. But it's easier to agree intellectually with the sentiment than to live it. Living it is very tough.

Sacrificial forgiveness is espoused by many of the world's major religions. In the New Testament Gospel of Matthew, Peter asks Jesus "How many times shall I forgive my brother or my sister who sins against me? Up to seven times?" and Jesus replies, "I tell you, not seven times but seventy-seven times." Of course, forgiving someone and giving them a second chance can be two different things— you may be able to do the former but not the latter. In any event you will push the other person to look at every possible solution by asking this question.

When to use the question
- When someone asks you for counsel about a difficult situation involving another person, or about a perplexing dilemma.

Alternative versions of the question
- When someone has done something wrong, or that is hurtful toward you, you can reverse the roles in yet another way. Ask, "If you were me, what would you do?" This may make the other person accept your decision more willingly.

Follow-up questions
- "Why do you feel that would be right?"

25 | How to Stop the Snorting

The phone call starts very badly.

On the line is my client and another senior executive at his firm, Bill. I have never met Bill before. He is angry. Apoplectic is a word that comes to mind. He's upset about how a major program is going. He thinks that bringing me in to fix it will only make matters worse.

"This is a mess," he shouts. "With all due respect, your suggested approach sounds redundant. I don't understand how it all fits together."

(Thank God this is a telephone call, I'm thinking to myself, and not a face-to-face meeting).

Bill alternately rants, grumbles, and criticizes for 25 minutes. He complains about the existing program they are trying. It isn't getting results. He sermonizes about their partners' complacency, and about how they are too internally focused.

But he doesn't talk about the real issue, which is obvious. It's the revenue gap they face. He doesn't talk about where they should

127

go from here and exactly what it is the partners need to do differently.

I had agreed to participate in the call simply to be helpful to my client. "No good deed goes unpunished," said the actress and congresswoman Clare Boothe Luce. This one certainly isn't exempt from that cynical admonishment.

With five minutes left, I gently interrupt: "Bill, can I ask you a question?"

"Well, sure," he snorts.

"As you look at your young partners, when you think about what it takes to build great client relationships—what do you wish they would do *more* of?"

There is silence.

He sputters, "Well . . . good question." Then a pause. "Oh, heck, you've gotten me off track now!" he exclaims. His voice is tinged with irritation at having had the pleasure of his rant cut short. After one more pause he adds, "Umm . . . Okay, let me address that."

Then he starts talking about the positive side of the change he wants to see: "Well, they need a roadmap, kind of like the one you e-mailed me. Yes, starting at the top of the page—I like this, I think there are three key things they need to do better."

His blustering stops and his anger recedes. Suddenly, as if by divine command, the storm is calmed and the waters are smooth and glassy. We're now having a real conversation about the underlying issues.

A few months later, I am starting a new major project with the company, authorized by Bill. Not because I sold anything, but because at the right moment I asked the right question.

A good question can be like an elixir that softens a bad mood, melts anger, and pulls the other person back to the truly important issues. When I asked Bill "What do you wish they would do more of?" I was able to take a derailed conversation and put it firmly back on the right track.

People often complain about others and insist that they need to change. You have to shift them from criticism to solutions by asking, **"What do you wish they would do *more* of?"**

Suggestions for How to Use This Question

"What do you wish they would do more of?"

They have to change!
    That's a common criticism. And criticism is contagious. If you can get the other person to be specific about the behaviors they wish to see, however, you'll achieve a powerful redirection of the conversation. You'll move from complaints and cynicism to productive dialogue about how to move forward. You will help sharpen the other person's understanding of the problem.
    Don't fix the blame, fix the problem.

When to use the question
- Whenever someone at work complains.
- When an individual is singled out and criticized.

Alternative versions of the question
- "If you could get your people to do just one thing differently—one action that would have a big impact on performance—what would it be?"
- "In what ways do you wish they would change?"

Follow up questions
- "Why do you think they aren't doing those things?"
- "Are they not doing the right things because they lack knowledge and skills, because the organization gets in their way, or because they don't have the natural ability?"

26 | Dig Deeper. Deeper. Still Deeper

"We're scheduling a training workshop for our sales executives. What would you charge to deliver a two-day training session?" On the phone is Kurt Dawson, the head of global sales for a company that makes industrial equipment.

(Whoa, I'm thinking. Hold your horses. I know I have to pull hard on the reins or this one will go places that don't make sense for this company or for me).

"Let's talk," I tell Dawson. "I can come by next week."

"Sometimes training isn't the best place to start," I add. "In my experience, there are times it's the very last thing you want to do." I can tell he doesn't like my response. He *wants* sales training. But is that what he *needs*?

Five days later I am sitting in Kurt Dawson's office, sipping burnt coffee from a 20-year-old coffee maker. He describes his company, products, and salesforce in glowing terms.

"We're the market leader. We have the highest quality in the business. Our salespeople are highly desired commodities—our competitors are always trying to steal them."

It sounds too good to be true.

I start with the first *Why*. I lean forward in my chair and ask, "Why do you want to do sales training?"

"Well, it's because we need to continually improve the skills of our salespeople."

I follow with the second *Why*. I ask him, "Why do you need to improve your salespeople's skills. It sounds like they are the envy of the industry!"

"I believe that if we improve their skills, they will be more effective at new client acquisition."

I go on to the third *Why*. "Why do you need to increase your new client acquisition efforts?"

He looks at me like I am asking why he needs to breathe air to stay alive.

"Our existing client base cannot support the growth targets our CEO has set for us. We need to bring in more new clients."

(Now we are getting closer).

I give Kurt my fourth *Why*. "And why can't you grow your existing clients fast enough?"

There is an awkward silence. He hems and haws for an eternity. I wait. I say nothing. (Never, ever interrupt a productive silence!).

"Well, it's the attrition. We are losing 20 percent of our existing clients each year."

I can almost hear a subwoofer pumping out that low, rumbling, dissonant chord that always accompanies the most frightening scene in every horror movie. It signals that something very bad is about to happen. Glenn Close is about to leap out of the bathtub at Michael Douglas in *Fatal Attraction*.

"Twenty percent." I repeat the statistic casually, with no judgment in my voice.

Finally, the fifth *Why*. "I just have to ask—why are you losing 20 percent of your clients each year?"

"We're being undercut by several competitors who are lowering their prices just to buy the business. But it's not sustainable. They cannot support such low prices for very long."

"And how do you know that?" I decide to press him even further.

"We survey our salespeople. And, I've heard this from a few clients as well."

(Finally, I've gone deep enough).

I tell my client that until we develop a better understanding of their attrition, their competition, and their clients' perspectives on their products and pricing, it makes no sense to put on a training program.

I persuade him to set aside the training program idea for now. Instead, I am engaged to conduct an intensive examination of their operations.

I interview the sales force, as well as some clients they've lost. The real problem quickly emerges. Dawson's company is only rarely getting undercut on price. Instead, there are significant quality and delivery issues with their products.

I confirm my original thinking. I tell my client that if they don't solve the quality and delivery issues first, the best training in the world will be a waste of time.

Because of the *five Whys* I have asked my client, the project we define together is much broader—and has far more impact—than a training program. I help Kurt lead a substantial effort to overhaul his company's operations, from production through sales. A client to this very day.

When someone says, "I want *this*," you have to find out what they really *need.* You do this by asking "Why?" You can ask this question as many as five times, starting with **"Why do you want to do that?"** or **"Why is this happening?"**

Suggestions for How to Use This Question

"Why do you want to do that?"

"Why?" can be a terrible question if used at the wrong time and for the wrong issue. It can communicate underlying disapproval. It can sound critical, carping, and nagging. It can make the other person feel bad about themselves.

"Why?" can also be a powerful question. It can make others think more deeply about what they are doing, and help them get to the heart of the issue. "Why?" can make us stop, reflect, and examine our actions instead of just mechanically going about our lives.

Use careful judgment in asking "Why?" but ask it often.

When to use the question
- When you genuinely want to understand someone's motivations.
- When the other person wants something but you're not sure they really need it.
- When you are trying to understand what are the root causes of a problem.

Alternative versions of the question
- "What result are you expecting from that?"
- "How did you decide to take that approach?"
- "Why do you think you should start there?"

Follow-up questions
- "Why is that?"
- "Why do you think that's happening?"
- "How do you know that?"

27 | Always Faithful

I want to tell you about one of the most remarkable men I have ever known. I'll give you the short version.

Thomas S. Monaghan is the founder of Domino's Pizza. He began in a room not much larger than most bedroom closets—a room 13 feet at its widest.

That was in 1960. The company grew from that one shop to more than 6,250 locations and 130,000 employees. He sold the company in 1998.

Domino's was privately owned by Tom and his family, so the exact amount they received in the sale is not public information. But I can tell you it was around a billion dollars.

He decided to sell so he could start a second career as a philanthropist. "I want to give it all away before I die," he said to me one day. (He's been pretty successful at that already. He figures he has given away somewhere between $700 to $800 million thus far.)

But this isn't the story about the fastest growing chain in the history of the United States at that time. That is another chapter for another time.

I want to tell you more about this extraordinary man. We're having dinner at his favorite restaurant. (No, we're not eating pizza!)

Tom is . . . well, Tom is what some would say a bit fussy about his food. No sauce on the fish, no starch, vegetables boiled with no butter or oil. His doctor says he'll live to be 100. Knowing Tom and his habits, I would bet on it.

He grew up in an orphanage. At the age of six, his greatest influence was Sister Berardo, one of the nuns at the orphanage. She said to him repeatedly during the day: "Tommy, be good, be the best you can be. Tommy, be good, be the best you can be." He has spent his life since then following that dictum. To be good and to do good.

In our many visits, I've probed and prodded. Tom is my hero. I've asked plenty of questions. I'll give you just a very small example of something I find interesting.

I've never seen Tom not wearing a suit. Always a green inner lining in the jacket. Almost always a green tie. (Well sure, of course: Monaghan. He's Irish.) I figure he gets up in the morning and showers with his suit on. One day I ask why he always wears a suit.

You need to know Tom is one of the most disciplined men you will ever meet. He lives by the code, by the book. His code, his book.

Back to the suit. He tells me that if you dress properly, you think properly. You act properly. You make better decisions. He tells me there is scientific proof. He had a dress code in his office of several hundred senior staff. Suits every day (no, they didn't need to have green linings). No sports jackets, no blazers. And a dress code for the women executives as well.

His business life and his philanthropic life have known peaks and some deep valleys. "In all the time I've known you, Tom, I've never seen you show any stress, no matter what the problem or challenge. How is that possible?"

"The only stress I know is when I'm lying on the couch and I realize the grass keeps growing and needs cutting. I credit my even mental attitude to prayer and exercise."

Would you like to know more about Tom? I think I'll write a book!

But first let me tell you about a question I ask him on this visit. His response is the most surprising I could possibly imagine. Totally unexpected. I find it absolutely amazing.

I ask Tom the same question I ask folks quite often: *What is the greatest achievement in your life?* It's truly a power question that always opens the mind and exposes the spirit of a person. It unlocks the prison of memories.

Are you ready for an answer you would never guess?

"Tom, what is the greatest achievement in your life?"

I expect him to tell me about starting what becomes the largest pizza chain in the world. No, that isn't it.

Or building and funding Ave Maria University, a great Catholic institution. And creating and supporting the Ave Maria School of Law. No, that isn't it.

Or how about his purchase of the Detroit Tigers and winning the World Series? That would be an extraordinary achievement. But that isn't it.

Or coming up with the idea of *Legatus* (Latin for Ambassador). This is the largest Catholic organization in the world for power leaders and CEOs of corporations. The group is committed to studying, living, and spreading the Catholic faith. That alone would gain him admission to anyone's hall of fame. But that isn't it either.

Reader, you will be surprised. I was, and I thought I knew Tom. Are you ready for his answer?

"Tom, what is the greatest achievement in your life?" I ask him.

"It was the day I applied to and was accepted in the Marine Corps. That was my greatest achievement."

"What?! Tom, of everything you have achieved in life, it's serving in the Marine Corps?"

"Yes. It taught me character, discipline, and values. It changed my life." From there we spend the next 30 minutes talking about his life-changing experiences in the Marines.

The Marine Corps motto is Semper Fidelis (Always Faithful). It seems to be ingrained in all who serve in this elite group. There is a life-long dedication and loyalty, a fraternity of comradeship that Marines have for the Corps and their country.

Do not be surprised if you get a totally unexpected response when you ask this question. That's because you will uncover the unfiltered psyche of the person you're talking with. You can count on that.

Oh, just a bit of unrelated trivia. You've seen the logo of Domino's. You have perhaps asked as I have—why two dots on one side and one on the other side of the domino? When Tom had just three shops, he asked an artist to design a logo. The three dots stand for the three shops that existed at the time. It continues to be the logo through all the years of growth.

To understand someone's inner being and learn what has been most important to them, ask: **"What is the greatest achievement in your life?"**

Suggestions for How to Use This Question

"What is the greatest achievement in your life?"

This question has many levels to it. It contains the potential to create deep, multi-layered conversations. It raises additional questions: Is it possible to define a single greatest achievement? Do we mean professional achievement or in any sphere, such as personal and family life? How do we define achievement, after all? It is a powerful question that provokes deep thought and dialogue.

Even if the other person has difficulty citing a single experience, you will learn a great deal about them. (And by the way, be prepared to answer this question yourself, as it may get quickly turned around on you!)

When to use the question
- When you want to deepen your relationship with someone and learn more about what is important to them.

Alternative versions of the question
- "What is your most personally gratifying achievement?"
- "What is the one achievement you are proudest of?"
- "In thinking about all of your achievements, which one do you think other people will most remember, and why?"

Follow-up questions
- "Say more about that. Why did you choose that particular one?"

28 | I Used to Be Indecisive— But Now I'm Not Sure

The meeting drags on. (As opposed to what?) I keep looking at my watch. Will it ever end? Tick tock.

This is a story this is quite likely familiar to you. You may even think I'm describing one of your own recent meetings.

It's a planning session for a major new initiative.

Three people arrive 15 minutes late. The rest of us sit around waiting, sipping coffee. The agenda is vague—"Discuss the 'customer-first' initiative launch." It's not clear exactly what the goal of the session is.

The conversation is obscured by the posturing and opinionated speech-making on the part of several of the participants. You know the type. Shallow brooks that run loud.

I try to give some focus to the meeting. This is getting painful. "What are we trying to accomplish?" I ask. I also ask the group questions such as "How will this impact your existing customers?"

The PowerPoint slides go up and down on the screen, like scaffolding that's being assembled, torn down, and reassembled again. I'm thinking: Why do people put slides up and then read them to you? Why does every thought produced in a corporation have to be laid out in a PowerPoint slide?

Our session ends at noon (mercifully, it was scheduled for only three hours). Someone says, "Let's make a list of next steps." Everyone nods. A sound idea. Isn't it good management practice to conclude every meeting with a list of to-dos?

The next steps all seem eminently practical. Cathy will call Bill to check on something-or-another. Roger will try and get so-and-so to support the program. Fred agrees to write up detailed meeting notes. Finally, I interrupt.

"May I ask a question?" Everyone nods again.

"What have we decided today?"

Hmmm. They look at me earnestly. "What do you mean?" one of them asks.

"I mean, what exactly did we decide? This was a planning session to help shape and structure a new initiative. So what did we decide? Can we make a list of those things—and then move to the to-dos?"

We make a list of five issues where we thought we had made decisions. Then we go around the table. We check for consensus.

It turns out there is no agreement about three of the five points. None at all. And one of those three points is about just what the primary goal of the program is! The problem is that corporate leadership kept talking about *multiple* goals when they announced the program. "Improve customer retention, cross sell more products, pre-empt the competition," and on and on.

Prioritizing these goals is essential to implementation. This is what I have to get across to the group.

We are making a list of kitchen utensils to buy but have neglected to put the floor and walls of the kitchen itself in place. No, it's worse. We're building a kitchen but aren't sure if it's meant for occasional cooking or to service 100 diners a day in a restaurant.

I tell them we still have work to do. We haven't focused on the real issues. We stay for another hour and a half, and finally have the real conversation we came together for.

We are now ready to leave the meeting. There is a list of the decisions discussed and agreed on. We are clear on the highest-priority goals. The action steps are there, too. But they are secondary to the *decisions made* and a reaffirmation of purpose.

Any group can make a list of next steps after a meeting. Decisiveness is rarer. And far more valuable.

Start creating a culture of decisiveness. Before you begin each meeting, ask, **"What decisions do we need to make today?"** After every meeting, ask: **"What have we decided today?"**

Suggestions for How to Use This Question

"What have we decided today?"

In many organizations, procrastination rules. ("I would do something about my procrastination—but I can't get around to it!")

People are afraid to make decisions. They are concerned about upsetting powerful, established interests. It's easier to play it safe than make a decision for which you may ultimately be accountable. Creating a list of benign action steps, which don't really take you anywhere important, is easy and low risk.

When you make decisions together, it binds the group with a public affirmation. The result is firm commitment to follow through on agreed action steps.

When to use the question
- After any meeting.
- After discussing an important issue with a family member or friend. ("So, have we decided anything?" or, "What have you decided to do?")

Alternative versions of the question
- *When someone comes to you with a problem or issue:* "Is there a decision that I need to make or that I can help you make?"
- *At the start of a meeting:* "What is the purpose of this meeting?" or, "What decisions do we want to make today?"

Follow-up questions
- "What is needed in order for a decision to be made on this?"
- "Do we all agree about that?"

29 | Blah Blah Blah

I have a dilemma.

Here's my problem. It's driving me crazy. I want to win the business. But I know deep down it's going to give me plenty of trouble. "The juice isn't worth the squeeze," as they say.

I'm discussing a project with a potential client who wants to control every aspect of my work. He wants to see excruciating detail for every methodology I mention. He wants to see my entire speech in advance. He insists he check the types of PowerPoint slides I will bring to the workshop with his people. There's a question about the precise percentage of expected group participation.

I am struggling with how to respond to his never-ending requests and directives.

I want the contract. But my gut tells me to run in the opposite direction. I'm getting more upset by the minute.

There's an expression in Italy, *Si vede il buon giorno dalla mattina.* (You can tell what kind of day it will be from the morning.) In other words, things often end the way they start. And this is not a good start.

I decide to consult my friend and mentor, author Alan Weiss. Alan is unusually skilled at parsing the issues and getting right to the point. He goes to the heart of things in a way that can border on brusqueness. It is sometimes painful but always liberating.

I call Alan. "I have a question I need to ask you."

"Okay, go ahead." There is no small talk. Alan gets right down to business.

"I have this prospective client. He's a senior executive with a large corporation in Chicago. It could be a very large contract. They are embarking on an ambitious program to drive revenue growth and create a more profit-oriented culture."

I continue on, giving more and more background on the client. "And furthermore, he wants to schedule call after call with me—including on weekends!"

I feel it's important to describe all this to Alan. No, essential! How can he possibly understand my problem, and give me suitable advice, without hearing the full context? I go on for several more minutes.

"Can I interrupt?" Alan asks.

"Of course," I tell him.

"What's your question?"

My flow is interrupted. I have plenty more information I still want to give Alan.

"Well, you see, this guy is feeling ownership of this program, and . . . " I start to restate the background information I know is critical to arriving at the right options.

Alan interrupts me again:

"What's your question? Five minutes ago you said you had a question. What is it?"

I'm beginning to squirm.

"The question? Hmm." I pause and think. "Okay, how do I deal with a client who is over-controlling and trying to micromanage me?" Alan chuckles.

"I knew there must be a question! Look, you don't tell them how to write the software that they sell to clients. And they shouldn't tell you how to consult. That's what you are an expert at.

You should tell your client that when you buy a Mercedes car you don't go into the showroom and insist that you fly to Germany to inspect the assembly line and make suggestions for how to manufacture your car. Mercedes is a great brand. You must trust the final product will meet high expectations.

"Similarly, tell them, 'you want to hire me because of my expertise, experience, and reputation in the marketplace. I have many years of experience at tackling similar problems, and you need to let me design this program in a way that will be most effective for you.'"

"Oh," is all I can muster.

"Are you still there?" Alan asks. "Does that answer your question?"

"Uh, yes, that's terrific. Thanks."

"You're welcome. Anything else?"

"No, this is very helpful."

"Call anytime."

I wanted to give Alan all the background on my problem—five or 10 minutes' worth. But in truth, most of it would have been unnecessary. I could have simply called up and said, "Here's my question." If Alan needed more information, he would then ask for it.

It probably happens to you often. A person says, "I want to ask you something." Then, they proceed to spend 10 minutes telling you every detail of a very convoluted situation they are enmeshed in. You do yourself and the other person a favor by getting them to focus on the true kernel of their issue. Simply ask: "What is your question?"

This question creates a powerful clarification for the other person. It's a bright yellow ray of morning sun that cuts through the fog.

When someone approaches you for advice and is vague or starts to give you too much background information, ask: **"What's your question?"**

Suggestions for How to Use This Question

"What's your question?"

This is a tough love question. People will resist it—often strenuously. But you must ask it.

When someone asks for advice or wants to "bounce something off you," you can help them immeasurably by asking this question. It forces them to crystallize their thinking. It makes them take the first step toward clarifying what the issue is and what advice they really need from you.

By asking this question, you'll also help reduce the amount of posturing that people do with you. You'll move faster toward an authentic conversation.

When to use the question
- Whenever someone says they have a question for you but then doesn't get around to asking it.
- When you're asked for advice, but the problem statement is so general that you really don't know what you're being asked for advice about.

Alternative versions of the question
- "There must be a question in there somewhere . . . what is it?"
- "What would you like me to give you advice about?"
- "You've mentioned several issues. What's the most important one you are struggling with?"

Follow-up questions
- "What have you tried?"
- "What do you think your options are?"
- "What's the thing you are you most concerned about?"

30 | Why Is This Day Different?

My good friend, Robie Wayneberg, invites me to dinner. A very special dinner.

He asks me to join him and his family in celebrating their Seder. It is the highly festive Passover dinner that commemorates the exodus of the Jews from Egypt. Passover is the most commonly observed and best known of the Jewish holidays.

It enjoys a rich, spiritual kinship to the Christian faith. It is believed that Jesus and His disciples gathered for the Seder on the last evening they were together. It's what we now call the Last Supper.

Robie's family gathers around the dining table. They give me a yarmulke to wear. I become a member of the family.

It is a deeply moving evening. The ritual begins. Three matzohs, the unleavened bread. The bitter herbs. The egg. The salted water. Then the roasted lamb and wine.

And then, one of the most soul-provoking questions I have ever heard. Become me for a moment. Get a front row seat at this scene. Think of the evening. The family. The ritual. The story of the flight from Egypt. And now the question.

"Why is this night different from all other nights?"

In some ways, it is actually close to the kind of question I've been asking for years. When my young kids were tucked into bed each evening, I would ask: "What made this day more special than any other day in your life? What were all the wonderful things that happened to you today?"

These questions made everything fade away that might have happened during the day that was negative. The snubbing, falling in the playground, the tough multiplication exercises, not being picked for a team, being caught chewing gum. All this would be forgotten.

Instead, the kids would recall a special moment. Answering correctly when their teacher called on them. Getting an extra ten minutes at recess. Spending time with their best friend after school.

It's a great question. *What made this day more special than any other?* My young kids are now grown with families of their own. They ask their children the same question.

I often still ask that very question when I'm talking with someone individually or in a group. Sometimes, I hear about a promotion at work, or a success with a customer. Often, someone relates a very small thing that brought great joy. It may have been a smiling child, an incandescent sunset, or an intimate conversation with their spouse.

It's magical. It's not unlike the stars of the sky whose beauty increases when they are studied for a long time, and new stars are discovered.

The question momentarily stops a person. It is, as Robert Frost writes, "at the threshold of discovery." The wheels begin turning. And then come the joy and a smile.

Try it. Ask the question at your dinner table. If you're lucky enough to have young kids still at home, ask it when you're tucking them into bed. Ask it of some of your friends. You will find sparkling moments of high happiness and rapture when the soul is laid bare.

If the description of a power question is one that is thought-stretching and calls for a response, this is indeed a question packed with punch and vigor. Mystical magic.

Dylan Thomas writes of being touched by life and etched in fire. That's it! That's it exactly. "What made this day more special than any other?"

Invite others to share their most treasured moments with you. Help them relish and savor their days by asking, **"What made this day more special than any other?"**

Suggestions for How to Use This Question

"What made this day more special than any other?"

This is an extraordinary question to ask over dinner, when entertaining friends at a cocktail hour, or with the family at the close of the day. The responses are almost always positive. People stretch to think of all the good things that have transpired. What makes this reaction special is that when joy overflows their cup, it tends to spill over onto everyone else.

Should the day's tidings be negative—and this doesn't happen often—just be aware that there are no rainbows without a cloud or a storm. Tomorrow will be a better day. In either case, the question leads to revealing discourse.

When to use the question
- At the end of any day, when you are talking to just about anyone!
- When someone has come back from a trip, adventure, or outing.

Alternative versions of the question
- "Would you tell me about your day?"
- "What happened today that made you smile? Did anything make you frown?"

Follow-up questions
- "Why was that particularly special for you?"

31 | Never Too Late

"This was a tough one," Roger explains to me. "I wasn't sure how to handle it."

"Tough? How?" I ask. I am amazed. "I've never seen you intimidated by meeting anyone. I can't imagine you being at a loss for words."

I want to hear more. Roger is one of the most confident, intelligent, and savvy consultants I have ever met. And he is no ordinary consultant.

After graduating as a Baker Scholar from Harvard Business School, he worked for 15 years at one of the most prestigious consulting firms in the world. Then, he left to be CEO of a large division of a Fortune 100 company. After five years of honing his leadership skills in the corporate world, he returned to his consulting firm, where he is now a senior partner.

Roger possesses a rare blend of relationship skills and analytical rigor. When he works with clients, he doesn't demonstrate the "sometimes wrong but never in doubt" confidence that some consultants flaunt. Rather, he exemplifies the "I know what it's like to walk in your shoes" understanding and empathy that only comes with 30 years of experience.

"So tell me the story. What happened?" I ask. Roger sits back, and takes another sip of coffee. I lean forward in my chair, pen and notepad in hand.

"A company engages us for a major strategy development project. It is very high profile work. We are three months into the engagement, and I have a meeting coming up with the CEO.

"I have met him several times before, but they were just brief discussions. This time we will be one-on-one, and I will have ample time."

"This sounds like a great setup. Go on!"

"You have to understand who this man is. He's an intimidating figure, six foot eight inches tall with striking blue eyes the color of a robin's egg. He has an encyclopedic memory. He never forgets a conversation or anything he reads. I've never met an executive who has such a complete command of his company's operations."

(I'm thinking, I'm glad it was Roger and not me. This is like General Robert E. Lee meeting Field Marshall Bernard Montgomery to discuss battle strategies).

"He was raised in an *orphanage*. Blessed with a sharp intellect and a powerful work ethic. He went to an Ivy League college and graduated *summa cum laude*. He worked his way up from an entry-level job at a manufacturing plant to become chairman and chief executive officer. Now, he is just a few years away from retirement.

"The problem is . . . I am struggling to come up with something truly compelling to say to this CEO. What intelligent statement can I make or insightful piece of information can I furnish that will demonstrate I am a worthy advisor to his company?

"After thinking about it for days, I realize that *nothing* I can tell him from our strategic analysis will be stunning or original. We are doing great work, and have lots of interesting findings. But I don't feel that part of our conversation will truly stand out.

"I decide I need to ask him a compelling question. But what can I ask him that won't come across as contrived—or at best, something he hasn't already heard from 10 other people?"

"So, what did you come up with?"

"Sometimes the best questions are simple, direct, and help you connect on a personal level. So, my briefing on the project ends. The small talk begins to die down. I take a deep breath. Then I say to the CEO:

"'William, I'd like to ask you something.'

"'Of course, go ahead,' he replies.

"'You've had an extraordinary career. You have accomplished so much, starting at the very first rung of the ladder, on the manufacturing floor. I'm guessing you've lost count of your many well-deserved awards and accolades.'

"The CEO smiles. I think I have touched the right button. He gives me begrudging acknowledgment and nods his head.

"'As you look ahead—is there something else you'd like to accomplish? Is there a dream you've yet to fulfill?'

"He pauses, looks straight at me. His eyes pierce me through. He becomes lost in thought for a few seconds. Then he slowly replies, 'You know, Roger, over many years I've collaborated closely with my board of directors. I've worked with lots of investment bankers and consultants, and with several large foundations I am engaged with. I've been involved with all sorts of smart and successful people. But no one has ever asked me that. Nobody ever asked me that question. *Nobody.*'

"The room is still. 'Yes, I do have something in mind. . . . ' he begins.

"Our meeting, which is due to end at noon sharp, ends up taking another half hour—an eternity on a CEO's tight schedule. More importantly, our relationship, which is strong to this day, really begins to develop after I ask that question."

I'm dying to hear what Roger's client tells him. But it has to wait.

"Now, the actual substance of what he wants to do after he steps down as CEO is also fascinating," Roger continues, "but it's not actually the main point of this story. This story is about the question—about asking someone, at just the right moment, 'Is there something else you'd like to accomplish?' It's about connecting with their dreams."

Compliment a client, colleague, or friend on their achievements. But don't stop there. Draw out their deepest, most heartfelt aspirations. Ask: **"Is there something else you'd like to accomplish? Is there a dream you've yet to fulfill?"**

Suggestions for How to Use This Question

"Is there something else you'd like to accomplish?"

Almost everyone has an unfulfilled aspiration or dream, no matter where they are in their career or their life. Rarely, however, do others invite them to share it.

Anyone can carry on a conversation about plans, reports, and recommendations. Go deeper and create a sublime moment by asking this question.

When to use the question
- When you've already had the chance to meet the other person a few times, and want to start to deepen the relationship.
- At any stage of someone's career.
- With a leader who will be stepping down in the next few years.

Alternative versions of the question
- "Is there a dream you've yet to fulfill?"
- "Do you have something in mind for your next act?"
- "After this, is there a particular challenge that excites you?"
- "What are your most important aspirations for your career?"

Follow-up questions
- "What will the timing of that be?"
- "Do you think that will stretch you in a different way?"
- "If you do go in that direction, what's the next step you'll take?"

32 | Take Stock of Your Life

It was one of the most exciting and memorable days of my life. I'll tell you the story. It begins with a telephone call.

"May I have the telephone number for Peter Drucker in Claremont, California?" I'm on the line with the long distance operator.

(I don't believe I can really get to talk with Dr. Drucker. I assume there is an answering machine or a gatekeeper. Still, I think I'll try. I am trying to reflect Melville's comment in *Moby Dick* that all people of action will find their way, sooner or later, to success.)

"Do you want Peter F. Drucker?" I don't really know his middle initial, but I assume there couldn't be too many Peter Druckers in Claremont. I tell her that's the one. She then says, "Is it the one who lives at 847 Marchand Street?"

"Hmm . . . yes, I believe that's the Drucker I want." The next voice I hear is Peter Drucker. Even though he has been in this country for 50 years, there remains the very heavy Austrian accent.

I explain to him that I'm calling because of a book I'm writing on the passion and commitment that directors of nonprofit organizations should bring to their board membership. I tell him I was hoping to get a quotation, a few sentences, I could attribute to him in my book.

Peter Drucker is still considered to be the world's foremost pioneer in management theory. He was a renowned author, teacher, and consultant. There is likely no single person in history who had a greater influence on the development of modern corporate and nonprofit management practice.

I tell Dr. Drucker that I am writing a book about board management for nonprofit organizations. "There is no one in the country who knows more about corporate boards than you," I explain. "I feel there are important similarities between a corporate board and a nonprofit board. I would like your views on this topic. When would be a good time to call you back?"

"That's fascinating," he says. "I'm also writing a book right now about nonprofit boards. Maybe you could come and visit me. We could kick it around for a while."

Good grief! I'm kicking it around with Peter Drucker.

"Would it be possible that you could visit me in Claremont on a Sunday?" I jump at the suggestion. After all, Claremont is only 3,000 miles away! We decide on a Sunday three weeks away.

I arrive at the Ontario, California, airport, rent a car, and am on my way to Marchand Street. I ring the bell at his modest home at precisely nine o'clock.

Dr. Drucker is dressed in an old plaid shirt, open collar.

"Come in. I've been looking forward to seeing you. My wife has made some coffee. Let's go in the kitchen and talk."

I have the whole day with my hero. I am taking notes as fast and furiously as I possibly can. I actually fill two complete pads of paper. A few months later, we have a full afternoon together as well. But that's another story.

One of our most significant discussions is about what Dr. Drucker calls "the five most important questions." I am embarrassed to tell you that I only manage to take down four of the questions.

I am daunted by his presence and don't want to interrupt. I am able to recall later what the fifth question is. I'll tell you about that in a moment.

"There are five questions that are essential for a board to consider," he says. "To be successful as an organization you must have thoughtful, clear answers to these questions. I'll walk you through each one of them."

(Now back to you, the reader. These questions are equally consequential to you on a personal basis. For our purposes here, I am going to explain how meaningful and valuable they are to you as a *person*.)

First, Drucker tells me that we must consider the mission of the organization. I am convinced it is equally important for a man or woman to have a personal mission statement. I've done it myself. It can be intimidating.

In your personal mission statement, answer these questions: Who am I? What values do I consider most important? What do I stand for? What do I want to achieve in life? How should I treat those closest in my life? How do I want to be treated? What is the purpose of my life?

Think it through. Then write it down. The mission statement will help you determine who you are, *say* who you are, and *do* what you say.

When you finish your personal mission statement, you will know quite precisely why you were put on this Earth. It's what Hemingway wrote—that it strips you of everything you thought you knew about yourself. If you do nothing else, I urge you to work on the statement. Go ahead, peel back the layers.

Next, Drucker said you should know who your customer is. For you, personally, this means you must consciously define who you want to spend your time with. What kinds of men and women do you want to interact with? Do they reflect your values and interests? Do they fuel your energy, your excitement for life?

Drucker goes on to tell me the third question: "What does the customer value?" On a personal level, this means you must understand what is important to all of your friends, family, and colleagues. What are their goals and priorities? And what do they treasure in their relationship with you?

Maya Angelou said: "People will forget what you said to them. They will even forget what you did to them. They will never forget how you made them feel."

The last question I managed to keep notes on is, "What results do you expect?" In personal terms, substitute the word *expectations* for results.

Are the people around you clear about what your expectations are? If you have children, do they know what you expect? What about your spouse or partner? Your boss? Your employees or your colleagues? Do you know what these same people expect from *you*? Have you ever asked them what they need?

The fifth and final question is the one I originally failed to write down. Perhaps this happened because Drucker mentioned it at the end of the most stimulating day of my life. My head was exploding with new ideas and excitement.

This final question is, "What is your plan?" This is as equally applicable to your personal life as it is to an organization. You've clarified your mission, what you stand for. You are clear about the people you want to invest in a relationship with. You have developed a deep understanding of what each person values, of what is important to them. They know what to expect from you and what you expect from them.

Your final step is to identify your plan—the short, medium, and long-term actions that will get you to where you want to go. Without a plan, you may go just about anywhere. Or nowhere.

There you have it, Peter Drucker's most important questions— hailed as the most consequential examination ever posed by a writer. Use these questions to guide you. To push you. Ask them of others. Frequently.

Keep in mind what Helen Keller said: "Life is a daring adventure." Begin now with your mission statement.

Challenge yourself to your core. Ask yourself—and others— Peter Drucker's five questions about **Mission, People, Value, Expectations, and a Plan.**

Suggestions for How to Use Peter Drucker's Five Questions in Your Personal Life

1. What is your mission?
2. Which are the most important relationships you want to invest in?
3. What are the essential priorities and goals of those closest to you?
4. What are your expectations of the people around you, and what do they expect of you?
5. What is your plan?

The great management thinker Peter Drucker used to pose five questions to his clients, focusing on Mission, Customers, Value, Results, and a Plan. These clients were large corporations but also major nonprofit organizations like the American Red Cross and the Girl Scouts. During his questioning sessions, Drucker would shake up even the most confident CEOs.

Now, turn these questions onto your own life. Use them to challenge yourself. Make the implicit explicit. Take a moment to lower the water in the river, and examine what's really under the surface, what's lying on the exposed banks of your life. Do you want to be ruled by serendipity, or conscious and planned choices?

Use all of these questions when you are coaching or mentoring others. Use just one of them according to the situation. If someone is trying to build a key relationship, ask "Do you know what that person's priorities and goals are right now?" If the other person is in a leadership position— as either a professional or a parent—ask "Do others know what you expect of them? Have you made that clear?"

33 | The Heart of the Matter

When someone's leg and knee begin bouncing up and down, the eyes wander, and the person has no questions—it's time to do something. You're in trouble.

I'm meeting with Kathleen, the co-chair of a large professional services firm. Our session was set up weeks earlier. The agenda is to review progress on a project I am doing for her company. I had prepared carefully, and had brought Kathleen a crisp briefing document. It summarizes our progress. It is clear and succinct. The paper is a heavy, impressive stock.

About 20 minutes into the discussion, I realize I have lost Kathleen. She just isn't there. She's fidgeting. She isn't asking good follow-up questions. It gets worse. She is starting to eye her BlackBerry.

You know that look. You dread it. The other person tries to show they are listening to you as they glance furtively down at their lap, where their smartphone is cradled. Kathleen's mind is somewhere else.

I pause, and let about five seconds pass—an eternity when you're sitting with a busy executive.

"Kathleen," I ask, "What's the most important thing we should be discussing this morning?"

She sits upright, suddenly more alert.

I wait.

"Hmmm. Well," she slowly begins, "this is helpful, getting your update. I value this summary and the suggestions you're making. It's very well done."

"Good, thank you. But we've got another 30 minutes scheduled together. What should we focus on?"

My client looks up at me, frowning and shaking her head. She sighs. "I just don't think my team is on board. They aren't getting it."

"Say more about that. When you tell me, 'they are not on board,' what symptoms are you seeing? What's not working?"

We shift gears. The next half hour we spend talking about the issues with her team. I ask several more power questions, and Kathleen reveals still more about the situation. I suggest some preliminary ideas to get her team better aligned with the strategy. We leave the rest of the project update for another occasion.

The tidy briefing package I prepared barely saw the light of day. It probably got what it deserved.

As I get up to leave, Kathleen asks me, "Can we regroup next week on this? You are asking some very good questions, and your suggestions are excellent. I want to chew this over a bit more with you."

Fast-forward. Based on the germ of our conversation six months ago, Kathleen is making some far-reaching changes to her top team. She also engages me to work with them one-on-one to improve their effectiveness.

When I asked, "What is the most important thing we should be discussing today?" this simple, direct question helped set

Kathleen on a path to improve her organization. It also deepened my relationship with her and her senior team.

When time is spent together on issues that are truly important to both parties, the relationship deepens and grows. There is increased emotional resonance. You become more relevant to each other. Bonded.

A CEO I consulted with several years ago told me something I have never forgotten. It is the key to being relevant.

"Remember," he said, "When you're considered part of a client's growth and profits, they will never get enough of you. But when you're viewed as just a cost to be managed, they can cut you anytime."

You must connect with the other person's agenda of essential priorities and goals. Then you will be seen as part of growth and profits. As an investment, not a cost.

When the other person is distracted or disengaged, or when you just feel you are not talking about their highest priority issues, you must ask: **"What's the most important thing we should be discussing today?"**

Suggestions for How to Use This Question

"What's the most important thing we should be discussing today?"

If what you are talking about does not align with the other person's most urgent priorities, they are going to wish they were elsewhere. You will dramatically increase your relevance and influence if you spend *more* of your conversations focused on what is *most* important to the other person.

When to use the question
Here are some occasions when you may need to refocus the discussion:

- In update meetings with a client or your boss.
- When making a sales pitch.
- With your spouse or significant other.

Alternative versions of the question
- "What would you like to talk about today?"
- "What's on your mind?"
- "We've got 20 minutes left . . . is there anything we haven't covered that we ought to discuss today?"
- "What aren't we talking about that we should be addressing?"

Follow-up questions
- "Can you say more about that?"
- "What's behind that?"
- "Why is this important to you now?"

34 | Capture the Moments

He had everything to live for.

There was a baronial home in Connecticut's most affluent zip code, a loving family, a salary beyond anything he had ever believed possible. And a recent promotion.

Let me tell you about the job. He was the CEO and Chairman of the Board of KPMG, one of the premier and largest accounting firms in the world. It was a position he had sacrificed to achieve. The long hours, the travel, neglecting the family, the scrambling to get the key position.

Gene O'Kelly was sitting on top of the world.

Then he discovers he has a blind date with destiny. On a routine semi-annual executive physical exam, he complains to his doctor about a reoccurring problem he is having. They probe and examine. The clinic puts him through a battery of extra tests.

The results are conclusive. The news is not good. Tragic.

Gene O'Kelly is told that he has an inoperable brain tumor. At best, he has 90 days to live. These are the moments you realize that life goes by so fast, if you don't stop every once in a while to look around you, you might miss it.

We don't know of the sudden despair he must have felt. How he broke the news to his wife. How he faced up to the prognosis. What middle-of-the-night fears he faced. In times like this, one's life shrinks or expands in proportion to one's courage.

What we do know is that O'Kelly was a driven man, compulsive, and a realist. He must have felt at some point, soon after his death sentence, that his 90 days of life were too precious to waste on regrets. He knew from his business experience that successful people are those who are good at moving to Plan B.

He decides to keep a journal chronicling the 90 days of life left to him. (Actually he will live 60 days beyond that.)

Now, please get a pen and paper. I'll wait.

I want to strongly suggest that you get a copy of the book he wrote. It's called *Chasing Daylight*. It made an indelible impact on me. It will on you, also. That's a promise.

It made me realize that I must look at things as if I am seeing them for the first time, but, also, as if I am seeing them for the last time. And perhaps as if I would never see them again. I had to take everything in and remember it all forever. I had to capture every moment.

I speak at workshops, seminars, and conferences. I spend about 60 days a year in my speaking engagements. Some years more.

The book made such an impact on me that I started beginning all of my speeches by asking the group to think about what they would do if they only had 90 days to live. Who would you visit? What wrongs would you right? Which friends would you tell how much you love them? What places might you want to visit for the last time? How would you spend the last days with your family?

You get the idea. I want to impress on those in my audience that life is a very fragile thing. You begin dying the day you are born. I remind them to live life to its fullest—their cup overflowing with joy, fulfillment, and rewards. I tell them to work as if they will live forever, and live as if they would die tomorrow.

After doing this exercise for a year or two, I realized that there was actually a more significant question. *What would you do if you knew you had only three years to live?* The reason that's a more consequential question is that it is more thought-provoking. It really stretches you.

Ninety days gives you an opportunity to quickly bring all of the elements of your life into a neat package and tie it with a ribbon. But changing the time frame to three years creates a very different challenge. It forces you to do a great deal more thinking and planning. It gives you time to do more than just wrap things up. You are reminded that things don't change. You change your way of looking at them.

You take a careful look at the inevitable forward motion of life. But suddenly it has an abrupt stop. The end.

The more I think about extending the time period to three years, the better I like the idea. That's when I decide I will do something a bit different at my speaking engagements. I do it now at all of them.

I give everyone a blank envelope. I tell them to write their return address in the left-hand corner. Then I have them address the envelope to themselves. "Mark it *Personal and Confidential,*" I tell them. In the right-hand corner where the stamp goes, I have them put the date.

I now ask them to write a quick narrative. A very special document.

"Don't worry about the sentence structure, spelling, or ending the sentence with a preposition. Forget everything your freshman English teacher taught you. What I want is a free flow of spontaneous writing.

"Make your mind into a blank sheet of white paper. Now you're ready to write.

"You have three years to live, three years from today. What would you do to change your life, personally and professionally? What would you hope to accomplish? Who are the people you would want to bring into your life in a more intimate way?"

I tell them that a friend is someone who knows the song of your soul and sings it back to you when you've forgotten the words. Who are those friends and why aren't you seeing more of them now? How would you change your life?

I give them 15 minutes to complete the narrative. No one really needs longer than that. I want an unadorned, unvarnished, and a totally *heart-exposed* report.

I ask them to fold the paper, put it in the envelope they've addressed, and seal the envelope. I gather all the envelopes and take them back to my office. I have these on a tickler. The office sends them out three years later.

I have been doing this now for about six years. The results are extraordinary. I have a dozen or so phone calls every month from folks who receive their envelopes.

They tell me that when they first see the envelope, it seems to them that the writing looks very familiar, but they can't remember having addressed the envelope. (Three years is a long time.) They open the envelope and read how they planned to spend the three years. That's when I get the phone calls.

Some tell me how close they are to being able to achieve what they had written. Many tell me how blessed they are to have lived beyond the third year. I have had glorious comments. I have made a note of all of them. (I think someday I'll write a book!)

Social scientists tell us that when you make a public commitment to something, it greatly increases the odds you will actually do it. We know that if you put it in writing, it leaves an indelible mark on your mind.

Just be careful what you wish for. It may very likely come true.

This is a question that can be used in countless situations. I have used it with clients, with friends, and the family. *"If you knew you had only three years to live, what would you hope to achieve personally and professionally?"*

It is a question that will lead you on a journey of wondrous pathways. The signposts are all down. There's no road map to follow.

This question forces people to begin thinking about how to re-order the priorities in their life. It helps them understand they must not wait until just the right time. The time will never be just right.

They will be ignited somehow by an emotional spark. The canvas of their life is neutral but the details are ready to be filled in and will be fluorescent.

Invite someone to think deeply about their priorities in life and how they want to spend the remainder of their days. Ask: **"If you knew you had only three years to live, what would you hope to achieve personally and professionally?"**

Suggestions for How to Use This Question

"If you knew you had only three years to live, what would you hope to achieve personally and professionally?"

Carpe diem has now become a cliché. Latin scholars say it may be translated as "seize the moment."

Cliché or not, it is a command that must drive and propel us. It tells us to embrace the whole of life. It is the hymn we sing. It encourages us to besiege the opportunity. To wage war on it.

You must engage the day, ravish the moment. Wrest and wring from life all that is good and all it will yield. Your objective should be to die young—as late as possible.

That is why this is such a powerful question. If you knew you only had three years to live, how would you spend the time? You will uncover unexplored, unexpected responses no other question elicits.

Carpe diem. That says it all.

When to use the question
- With your friends, family, business colleagues, and just about anyone you know.
- To shake up other peoples' thinking and pull them out of the day-to-day minutia of their lives.

Alternative versions of the question
- "What are the most important things in your life? Are you spending enough time on them?"

Follow up questions
- "What's stopping you from doing this—now?"

35 The Awe and Wonder of the Power Question

Come with me. We're going to Bossier, Louisiana. It's some time in the 1950s.

Madeline tells Bonnie, age eight, and her six-year-old sister, to come out to the backyard. Madeline is their mother. "Bring a sheet of paper and a pencil with you," she tells them.

There's Madeline sitting on the ground. You can see her there with a shoebox and a small shovel next to her. The girls sit on the ground next to their mother.

"Now dig a hole." They dig a hole big enough for the box to fit in.

"Now write the word *can't* on the slip of paper you brought with you. Fold it and put it in the shoebox. Then we'll bury the box.

"Now," Madeline says, "you'll never be able to say the word *can't* ever again." That's been Bonnie's credo ever since: Never say "I can't."

Fast forward to Bonnie's teenage years. She refuses to learn to sew. That's really what set the stage for her later years.

Bonnie thought she would study to be a fashion designer. Then the school handed her a needle and thread. She was told she would have to learn to sew if she wanted to be a fashion designer. That was the sudden end of what would have been an unpromising career.

Thank goodness. I believe we saved the world from having a mediocre designer.

Bonnie McElveen-Hunter instead ended up heading and owning the largest custom publishing company in the United States. It is one of the largest woman-owned businesses in the nation.

She has somehow managed all this and, in addition, served as U.S. Ambassador to Finland. There's more. She is the first female Chair in the history of the American Red Cross. Bonnie is a roaring advocate for women and created the International Women's Business Leaders Summit.

I once sat next to General Colin Powell at dinner. It was at a national meeting of the Urban League, where he was being honored. He had just retired as Secretary of State. He had sworn Bonnie in as Ambassador. I told him I knew Bonnie.

"She's amazing," he said. "She is the brightest and one of the most exciting people I know. She is tremendously effective. Energy personified."

I'll tell you how I think of Bonnie. I've chosen a Finnish word: *sisu*. It's the desire for that special extra within you that impels something amazing and extraordinary. To me, that perfectly characterizes Bonnie's drive and vitality. When others think of what's impossible, Bonnie starts counting the possibilities.

I've known and worked with Bonnie for more than a dozen years. She's an inspiration. I've learned to use a new word regarding my feeling for her. Bonnie is my *s/hero*.

Over the years and during the course of dozens of conversations with her, I have asked a number of power questions. They would test anyone's thinking and help promote a flood of conversation.

For instance, I remember one luncheon we had. I asked her, *What is the most profound and difficult question you have ever been asked?* She paused, but only for a moment.

"Someone once asked me, 'What difference will your footsteps make a hundred years from now?'" (I'm reminded that a good example is the best sermon.)

Then Bonnie spends the next 10 minutes or so talking about how she hopes to make a significant difference in her lifetime that will have an impact for generations to come.

One power question. A 10-minute response.

There is another time we were visiting together. "Bonnie," I said, "*What is the most profound and difficult question you have asked someone?*" That's a question that will likely stir anyone's thinking.

She tells me about a meeting she had with the Palestinian Red Crescent Society and Magen David Adom (Israel's emergency medical and disaster service—its answer to the American Red Cross). It was regarding a merger of the International Federation of Red Cross and Red Crescent Societies.

"I asked them, 'What really are the differences between the Red Cross and the Red Crescent Societies?' We struggled for an hour to try to determine if there were any differences. There weren't. I also asked leaders of the Red Cross the same question.

"Let's get to the heart of the issue. I ask, 'Isn't the love that we share for humankind greater than the chasm of difference that manifests daily and tests civility?'"

On another day I'm in Bonnie's office. People are dashing in and out—checking in, asking questions, wanting decisions. The flow died down long enough for me to ask, "Bonnie, *What is your idea of a perfect day?*"

"That's easy. A perfect day for me is any day I am vertical . . . and any day in which God *disturbs* me to move outside the normal noise of my life and serve a greater purpose."

I follow that with this question, *"What has been the greatest day in your life?"* I'm on a run and I have her undisturbed attention.

"I believe my greatest day is yet to come. That's when I hope to hear those seven most precious words, *Well done, my good and faithful servant.*" I spent the next 30 minutes listening to Bonnie's response to these two questions.

There was another visit. "Bonnie, you have already achieved so much in life. If there were a National Women's Hall of Fame, you would be one of the first to enter. You are among a handful of the top women in this country. *How would you like to be remembered?*"

"I'm still working on that. But I'm reminded that we come into this world with nothing, we're leaving with nothing, and all we ever really keep . . . is what we've given away. I'd like to be remembered as someone who has given herself away.

"I want to be remembered as a person who gave encouragement and inspiration so that others could reach their full potential." That comment leads to another 15 minutes or so of bright and amazing discourse on Bonnie's feeling regarding what one must do in their life.

There is a bit of dogma in all of this. You'll forgive me if I preach a bit. Her life is ransomed to an unending commitment to serve.

I've told you the amazing story of this remarkable person. But I have only given you a few bits and pieces of her life.

I want you to understand, however, that this chapter is not about Bonnie McElveen-Hunter—as amazing as she is. The lesson here is about the capacity of potent and formidable questions to unleash a cascade of innermost feelings and vibrant conversation. Conversation that is intimate, personal, and memorable.

In this chapter, I write about many different questions I ask in separate visits. It illustrates how you can vary your questions, and use many of them, even if you have many meetings with a person. Asking a power question is not a one-off event!

The energy and vigor of power questions is your mightiest ally in drawing out deeply held feelings. When used at the right moment, they transform your conversations.

Power questions are important because they open the door to bottomless exploration and opportunity. Above all, they help you build relationships, win new business, and influence others.

Not Just
for Sunday

293 More Power Questions

The Power Questions So Far

The 35 chapters in this book highlight a series of power questions that can transform conversations and even lives. Before we move on, however, let's summarize the principal power questions you've just read about. If you count these together with some of the additional questions found in the chapters, and add those from the next section, we end up with at least 337 questions that you can use in a variety of situations.

Here are the main ones from the preceding chapters:

What would you like to know about us? (p. 11)
What do you think? (p. 16)
Are they ready to buy? (p. 22)
How will this further your mission and goals? (p. 25)

Socrates's questioning techniques (p. 31)

How did you get started? (p. 36)

Do you mind if we start over? (p. 41)

Why do you do what you do? (p. 46)

What in your life has given you the greatest fulfillment? (p. 51)

Is this the best you can do? (p. 57)

Is it a yes or a no? (p. 62)

Power questions that access goals and aspirations (p. 67)

What are your dreams? (p. 72)

What do you feel is the right decision for you? (p. 76)

What did you learn? (p. 82)

Can you tell me more? (p. 86)

What parts of your job do you wish you could spend more time on, and what things do you wish you could do less of? (p. 90)

What is the most difficult question you have ever been asked? (p. 95)

If you had to write your obituary today, what would you make it say about you and your life? (p. 102)

How do you see me as a leader? (p. 107)

What has been the happiest day in your life? (p. 113)

Can you tell me about your plans? (p. 119)

If the circumstances were turned around, how would you like to be treated? (p. 126)

What do you wish they would do more of? (p. 129)

Why? Why do you want to do that? (p. 134)

What is the greatest achievement in your life? (p. 139)

What have we decided today? (p. 144)

What's your question? (p. 148)

What made this day more special than any other? (p. 152)

Is there something else you'd like to accomplish? (p. 157)

Pete Drucker's five magic questions (p. 164)

What's the most important thing we should be discussing today? (p. 168)

If you knew you had only three years to live, what would you hope to achieve personally and professionally? (p. 174)

Power Questions Are Not Just for Sundays

In the chapters you just read, we described actual conversations in which power questions were used. We felt it essential to illustrate them with real-life examples. After all, a question that is part of a true and dramatic story becomes memorable, even indelible. You can see its impact.

But there are far more power questions than just those we wrote about. Many more. Thoughtful, probing, provocative questions you should be using every day—at work, at home, and with your friends. Even with strangers you meet on an airplane.

In this section, we share another 293 such questions. They are listed under nine topics to help you do the following things.

1. Win new business
2. Build relationships
3. Coach and mentor others
4. Resolve a crisis or complaint
5. Engage your leadership
6. Engage your employees
7. Evaluate a new proposal or idea
8. Improve your meetings
9. Ask for a gift

Use these questions to add zest and meaning to your conversations and to deepen your relationships.

We don't have a story around each question. That's now your job. Take charge. Use these questions to create your own touching, revealing, powerful stories.

1. Win New Business

What is the secret to winning a sale? To convincing a potential buyer to go with *you*?

A buyer is created when a clear need is identified, a trusting relationship is established, and value is demonstrated. The most successful salespeople in the world create these conditions by asking great questions.

They don't build their credibility with prospective buyers through fancy PowerPoint presentations. Instead, they use thoughtful, informed questions that implicitly demonstrate their knowledge and experience. They use questions to uncover hidden needs. To identify whether or not there is a problem or opportunity they can address. The best salespeople also use questions to connect on an emotional level—to get to know the other person and show they care.

It doesn't matter whether you're selling a product, a service, or an idea. When you first meet someone, power questions quickly earn respect for you. And that's the first step toward building a trusting relationship.

Holding Effective First Meetings

1. From your perspective, what would be a valuable way for us to spend this time together?
2. What would be useful for you to know about our firm?
3. What prompted your interest in our meeting?
4. In talking to my clients in your industry, I'm struck by a couple of particular issues they are grappling with. These include: [give examples]. How would these resonate with you and your management?
5. How is your organization reacting to . . . ? (a recent, important development in this client's industry or function)
6. How are you handling . . . ? (new competition, low-cost imports, a new regulatory framework, etc.)
7. Is there is a particular competitor you admire?
8. Can you tell me what your biggest priorities are for this year?
9. What are your most significant opportunities for growth over the next several years?

10. What exactly do you mean when you say . . . ? ("risk-averse", "dysfunctional", "challenging," etc.)
11. Who would you say are your most valuable customers?
12. What would your best customers say are the main reasons they do business with you?
13. Why do customers stay with you?
14. Why do customers leave?
15. When customers complain, what do they say?
16. How have your customers' expectations changed over the past five years?
17. How would you describe the biggest challenges facing your own customers?
18. What's the driving force behind this particular initiative? (What is behind the drive to reduce costs, design a new organization, etc.?)
19. What would "better" (risk management, organizational effectiveness, etc.) look like?
20. How did you reach the decision to seek outside help?
21. How much agreement is there, internally, about the problem and the possible solutions?
22. From your perspective, given everything we've discussed, what would be a helpful follow-up to this meeting?

Developing a Need

23. How much do you think this is costing you?
24. What do you think it's worth to fix this?
25. How is this affecting other aspects of your business? (sales, costs, productivity, morale, etc.)
26. How do you know that . . . ? (turnover is high, productivity is low, risks are not being well managed, etc.)
27. Who in your organization really owns this problem?
28. If an effective solution is found, how will it affect your own job?
29. Why is this important to you right now?
30. Is this one of your top three or four priorities?
31. How much time do you personally devote to this issue?
32. Can you give me an example of that?

33. If you do not address this (problem/opportunity, etc.), how might your business be impacted?
34. What solutions have you already tried and how successful were they?
35. What kinds of organizational resistance will there be to this change?
36. Is there anything I haven't asked about that you think is relevant to understanding this issue?

Understanding Aspirations and Goals

37. Where will your future growth come from?
38. How do you think your current strategy is going to change, given trends such as . . . ?
39. Why have you been successful so far? How will those reasons change in the future?
40. You've already reached some important milestones and accomplished an enormous amount. Where do you go from here in terms of future improvements in performance?
41. How much of your growth will come from existing customers versus new customers? What's your thinking behind that?
42. If you had additional resources, which initiatives would you invest them in?
43. Are there any things you need to de-emphasize or stop doing?
44. What more might you ask for if you were not afraid of getting "no" as an answer?
45. How would you say your priorities have changed over time?
46. How will your own performance be evaluated at the end of the year?
47. Are there any organizational or operational capabilities that you will need to significantly strengthen in order to support your future strategy?
48. What demands will your future strategy make on the quality and quantity of people that you need?
49. As you think about the future of your business, what are you most excited about?
50. As you think about the future of your business, what are you most worried about?

51. You've been very successful in your career. Is there something else you'd like to accomplish?
52. What are your dreams for the future?

Discussing a Proposal

53. We had planned to cover the following areas. What parts of our presentation will be most valuable for us to emphasize and spend time on?
54. Can you restate, in your own words, what you hope to gain from successful completion of this program?
55. Given what we've set out in our proposal, and thinking about value to you, can you say something about what you'd like to see more or less of?
56. What do you like most about the approach we've outlined?
57. What aspects concern you?
58. In what ways does this capture what you're trying to accomplish?
59. In thinking about choosing a partner to work with on this, what's most important to you?
60. May I ask, who else are you talking to?
61. Can you walk me through your decision-making process?
62. Who will make the final decision about choosing a firm to work with?
63. How will the funding for this be determined?
64. If two providers are evenly matched in terms of technical ability, experience, and price, how will you make your decision?
65. I sense you do have some hesitation. Can you help me understand what is behind that?
66. Is there anyone else who we ought to discuss this with or hear from before we finalize our approach?

Before Meeting with a Client: Questions to Ask Yourself

67. Have I thoroughly discussed the client's needs and expectations for this meeting?

68. If substantive information or recommendations are being presented, have we previewed these in advance with all the right constituencies?
69. Are the right people—from their side and from our side—coming to the meeting? Do I know who they are and how many there are?
70. If more than one of us is attending, have we discussed and clarified the roles that everyone is going to play?
71. What are the most prominent messages or ideas that I want to get across? How would I summarize these in one minute or less?
72. What are the different options for presenting our ideas? Can we use flipcharts rather than PowerPoint? Do we have some engaging stories that can help to illustrate our points?
73. Is there anything I can give to them beforehand (e.g., pre-readings) that will make this meeting more productive?
74. What's going on in this person's world right now? What pressures are they feeling (at work, at home, etc.)?
75. How will they react to what I have to say?
76. Is there enough flexibility built into the schedule to have a vibrant, give-and-take discussion, and/or to pursue other issues that the client may want to discuss?
77. What additional information do we need (about the individuals who will be attending, other important data, etc.) before this meeting?
78. What are the three or four thought-provoking questions that I plan to ask at this meeting?
79. What do I think will be the likely follow-up to this meeting?

2. Build Relationships

How do you move from an acquaintanceship to a meaningful relationship?

A relationship deepens when two people get to know each other better. This means you must share important experiences, reveal yourself personally, and connect on an emotional—not just professional—level.

Relationships are dynamic. They rarely stay the same. They either improve and evolve, or they wither on the vine. This particular set of questions will help you ensure that your relationships continue to grow, deepen, and prosper.

Connecting Personally

80. What would you like to be remembered for?
81. What has been your greatest accomplishment?
82. What has brought you the most fulfillment in your life?
83. What was the happiest day of your life?
84. What do you wish your younger self had known about (success, relationships, being a parent, etc.) that you know today?
85. Can you tell me something about your own career and how you got to your current position?
86. What do you like best about working for your organization?
87. In terms of your own effectiveness and how you spend your time, what would you like to do less of, and on which activities do you want to spend more time?
88. Tell me about your family. How old are your children?
89. When you're not shaking things up here at work, how do spend your free time?
90. What do you think about (a current event, the election results, or anything else)?
91. Who have been influential role models or mentors to you?
92. Where did you grow up? What was that like?
93. What were your parents like? What did you learn from them?
94. If you hadn't gone into (business, teaching, medicine, etc.), what do you think you would have done instead?
95. If you had to write your obituary today, what would it say?
96. What's the most memorable book (movie, concert, etc.) you have ever read?
97. Do you think you are an extrovert or an introvert? Why do you say that?
98. In thinking about e-mail, the telephone, written correspondence, face-to-face meetings, social media, and so on—how would you describe your communication style and preferences?

99. I don't know much about your early career—can you tell me about what you did during the first five years or so?
100. How did you get your start?
101. What do you think are your boss's most pressing issues right now?

Understanding the Other Person's Agenda

102. Can you tell me about your work? What kinds of activities take up most of your time?
103. At the end of the year, how will you be evaluated?
104. What is your organization looking for from you this year?
105. What are the major projects or initiatives you're working on?
106. What's important to you right now?
107. What are you most passionate about in your life right now?
108. What are the most important things you'd like to accomplish this year?
109. If you had a couple of extra hours in the week, what would you spend them on?
110. What are the favorite things you like to do when you're not . . . ? (at the office, taking care of your family, etc.)

Empathizing with Others

111. Tell me, how are you?
112. Can you say more about that? What's going on?
113. What do you mean when you say you're feeling . . . ?
114. Why do you think that happened?
115. How did you feel about that?
116. I'm trying to imagine what you're feeling. I think it's (angry, embarrassed, proud, etc.). Is that right?
117. How (angry, embarrassed, proud) would you say you are right now?
118. Was what happened difficult for you? I imagine it was challenging. [*Never be dismissive—take everything that's said seriously.*]

119. Do you feel that was the right thing to do? Or, Do you think that was the right response? [*Don't judge. Judgment stops empathy dead in its tracks. Ask the other persons what they think!*]

120. It seems like there are really two different issues going on here, is that right? Or, It seems like you feel stuck between a rock and a hard place . . . is that right? [*Paraphrase and affirm. Summarizing what someone has said is boring and tedious. Paraphrasing, or synthesizing, is far more powerful*].

121. What are you thinking of doing? Or, What do you think your options are?

122. I had a very similar experience. Can I share it with you?

123. Is there anything I can do that would be helpful?

Getting Feedback about a Professional Relationship

124. From your perspective, how do you feel our collaboration is going?

125. Could you give me an honest assessment of our work together?

126. Is there anything that you'd change about our relationship?

127. What should I be doing more of? Less of?

128. Are there individuals in the organization with whom I need to spend more time?

129. Is there sufficient communication so far?

130. Am I doing an effective job at linking our work to your key priorities?

131. What have I done that has been most helpful to you?

132. In what ways am I helping you to achieve your goals?

133. Do you feel I am working on the most central and critical issues for you?

134. How can I make your life easier?

135. How could I make doing business with me easier?

136. In what ways could I be a better listener to you and your organization?

137. Are there any aspects of your business or parts of your organization that you think I should understand better?

138. Overall, how can I do a better job of helping you to meet your own objectives?

139. Are there any other issues that we ought to be aware of or thinking about for you?
140. Do you have any other concerns that you'd like to put on the table?
141. On a scale of 1 to 10, how enthusiastically would you recommend me and my firm to a friend or colleague?

3. Coach and Mentor Others

Who in your life, right now, is benefiting from your experience and wisdom? Your age doesn't matter. Mentoring and coaching others is an extraordinary service you can provide, whether it is part of your professional or your personal life.

Power questions are especially valuable when you are coaching someone. They help you guide the other person to a solution rather than mandate a direction. They help you bring out the other person's hopes, fears, and dreams. Power questions enable you to challenge them in a way that is empowering rather than constraining.

142. How can I be of the greatest help to you in our relationship?
143. What's the best mentoring or coaching experience you've ever had? Why was it so effective for you?
144. What are your most important goals right now?
145. What questions are you grappling with now?
146. What questions can I help you answer?
147. What are you most excited about in your life right now?
148. Is there something that you feel is very difficult to do, but which, if you could do it, would substantially increase your success?
149. What is your time frame for achieving these goals?
150. What will you have to accomplish in order to get where you want to be?
151. What are you most afraid of as you think about trying to achieve these goals?

152. What are the most important obstacles you're facing?
153. Is there anything at all you can think of that would remove those obstacles?
154. Can you give me an overview of the problem? How did it get to this point?
155. What have you tried so far? How has that worked?
156. What's the best resolution to this that you can imagine?
157. Have you ever dealt with anything similar before? What happened in that case?
158. What don't you know in this situation that you wish you knew?
159. Can you give me an example of what you just stated?
160. Looking back, what have you been the most successful at? Why?
161. When can you remember being truly satisfied at work?
162. What parts of your work, today, are the most satisfying to you?
163. What are your greatest abilities?
164. What do you value most?
165. What are some of the things you need to let go of in order to move forward and accomplish your goals?
166. What is your dream for the future of your career?
167. What's been the most helpful to you in this conversation?
168. Based on this discussion, what do you see as your next steps?

4. Resolve a Crisis or Complaint

When someone complains, the first reaction often is to argue the point and try to show them that they don't have all the facts. To set them straight. You become intent on proving you are right.

When a person is upset, however, emotions are like facts. People want to be heard and understood. Rational argumentation will not win the day. Worse, it will inflame the tension. When there is a disagreement, your goal is to win the relationship, not the argument!

During the first phase of any crisis or problem situation, you must lead with questions. By doing so you will learn essential information and—most importantly—create an ally in solving the problem.

169. Thank you for raising this with me. Can you tell me everything you know about the situation?
170. Can you say more about that?
171. Really?
172. What happened then?
173. What has their reaction been?
174. How do you think it reached this point?
175. What else can you tell me?
176. I'm sorry this happened. What would you like to see done at this point?
177. This is extraordinarily important to me. How soon can we meet to discuss this in person?
178. Would it be helpful if I did some additional fact-finding, and then we could meet face-to-face in the next couple of days to discuss some proposed actions to address this?
179. If anything else surfaces in the meantime, can you let me know immediately?

5. Engage Your Leadership

What is it about someone's performance and attitude that instills confidence in their leadership?

Just as a client is impressed with strong, thought-provoking questions, your boss or organization's leadership will be too. Your capacity to handle your work effectively and achieve your goals is essential. But just as important is your attitude and outlook.

Are you a know-it-all? Or are you someone who exhibits a healthy curiosity and desire to learn? Are you a lone ranger? Or do you consult with your colleagues and superiors on a regular basis?

These questions will help you engage with your leadership and demonstrate the hallmarks of a truly curious and committed member of the organization.

180. What are the most critical initiatives for the organization over the next 12 months?

181. What are your own priorities for the next 12 months?
182. What does your boss expect from *you* this year?
183. In terms of accomplishing our goals, where are we on track or ahead of plan and in which areas are we behind?
184. Is there anything I can do to support you as you pursue your goals?
185. How can I be helpful to you as you make this decision?
186. How can I be helpful to you as you implement this decision?
187. Can you share with me how you and your leadership reached that decision? What other options did you consider?
188. What are the major challenges you see yourself facing in the future?
189. What gets you excited about the future?
190. As you look back over your career, what has characterized the outstanding performers who have worked for you?
191. From your perspective, what do you think my most important priorities should be in the short, medium, and long term?
192. If, at my next performance review, I wanted to exceed your expectations for me, what would I need to have done between now and then?
193. What do you think are my three greatest strengths? My biggest weaknesses or developmental needs?

6. Engage Your Employees

Great leaders ask great questions. They know that if *they* come up with all the answers, the chances of having anyone else buy into the solution are next to zero. But if their employees come up with the answer—if they feel ownership of it—there is a good chance it will bear fruit.

Telling, commanding, and stating the truth as you see it will not engage or empower. Answers make you feel like a leader, but questions create real followers.

194. Are we doing anything that is no longer important or effective and that we should stop?

195. What ideas do you have to help grow our organization?
196. How can we improve this?
197. What do you think is the single most important action we can take to make our organization more successful?
198. Do you know why we do it this way?
199. What do you think is the real problem at the bottom of this issue?
200. Is there anything getting in the way of your performing your job effectively?
201. What ideas can you suggest for . . . ? (reducing costs, growing revenues, improving productivity, improving innovation, etc.)
202. What would make your job more interesting and exciting?
203. Where would you like to go in our organization?
204. What additional information or resources would allow you to be more effective?
205. Where do you see me being the most effective and having the most impact?
206. What do you love most about your job?
207. What are the most challenging parts of your job?
208. Based on your experience, how would you describe the culture of this organization?
209. What makes you proud to work here?
210. Can you point to a recent management decision you didn't understand or wish you knew more about?
211. What could leadership do to communicate more effectively to the organization?
212. Who in our organization do you wish you knew better?
213. What are we hearing from our customers lately?

7. Evaluate a New Proposal or Idea

How do you determine whether a new idea is good or bad? If it has promise or if it is completely unrealistic?

Every day we are bombarded with ideas and proposals. Someone who reports to you at work may propose a new initiative requiring investment. Or, one of your children may have an idea about a new sport they want to take up or a career path they want to follow.

Whether you're talking to a client or a family member, these questions will give you the ability to learn, engage, and assess what they are proposing.

214. Why are you doing this? (What appeals to you about doing this?)
215. What is your mission?
216. What is important to you about this?
217. What are your most important goals?
218. What, specifically, do you hope to achieve?
219. What will the results look like?
220. What outcomes do you seek?
221. What will success look like?
222. How will this affect . . . ? (customers, employees, suppliers, support staff, or others.)
223. What changes do you think this will create?
224. Do you think there could be any negative consequences?
225. How could this limit your ability to act in other ways or other places?
226. What are your most important assumptions?
227. What are you assuming about . . . ? (any number of variables that may impact the decision.)
228. How could you verify that assumption?
229. What if one of your key assumptions is wrong?
230. What's your plan?
231. How are you going to approach this?
232. What help or resources do you need to accomplish this?
233. When do you plan to start?
234. What factors are governing your timing?
235. Are there advantages to starting sooner? Later? Disadvantages?
236. Who will decide or influence the timing?
237. What could go wrong?
238. What are the risks of waiting or doing nothing?
239. What are the two or three most important things that have to go well in order for this to succeed?
240. Which risks can you control, and which are uncontrollable?
241. What else have you considered?
242. If you had no constraints whatsoever, what would you do?
243. How does this compare to other alternatives?

244. What's the next-best alternative? Is there anything that could change to make that one look like the best alternative?
245. Is this consistent with your mission?
246. Is this consistent with your beliefs and values?
247. Is this consistent with what you've been saying publicly?
248. How consistent will this be with other initiatives that are going on in the organization?

8. Improve Your Meetings

At their worst, meetings are where you spend minutes and waste hours. Talk to anyone who works for a large organization (or a small one, for that matter) and you will hear about how much time is spent—and often wasted—in interminable meetings.

By asking these questions—starting with, "Is there an alternative to having a meeting?"—you will increase the effectiveness and productivity of the meetings you participate in.

249. What is the purpose of this meeting?
250. What do we hope to achieve?
251. Who else will be there or should be there?
252. How long does this need to be? Why?
253. Can we do this in 30 minutes? (rather than an hour.)
254. Is there an alternative to having a meeting?
255. What decisions do we need to make?
256. Do we know enough to make a decision?
257. What decisions have we made?
258. How do we feel this meeting went?
259. Was this a good use of our time?
260. Did we accomplish what we had hoped?
261. In retrospect, should we have held this meeting?

9. Ask for a Gift

We estimate there are more than 30 million men and women in the United States who serve on boards of nonprofit organizations. You may be one.

These directors and trustees carry as one of their major responsibilities the raising of funds for their organization. Here are a few power questions that you may use with someone you are calling on for a gift. What will flow is a stream of conversation that will help you get inside the heart and spirit of the person.

262. How do you feel we can most effectively serve our community (patients, students, the homeless, etc.)?
263. If you were the CEO and knew you could achieve any objective, what would you undertake for our organization?
264. How do you feel about the services of this organization? What would you suggest they do to expand their outreach?
265. How do you like to be told about the results of your gift?
266. When did it first occur to you that philanthropy was important in your life?
267. If you were a board member, how do you feel we could most effectively use your funds?
268. What would you change about our organization?
269. In what ways could we serve better and more effectively?
270. Why do you think we are one of the better-known organizations in our community?
271. How can we become even better known?
272. How can we do a better job of telling our story?
273. What qualities and attributes do you like best in the CEO of our organization or of another organization that you know and work with?
274. You're a graduate of our college. In what way have we helped you prepare for life?
275. How important is recognition to you?
276. What is your idea of perfect recognition for a gift?
277. How do you like to be thanked for your gifts?
278. What has been your experience with our organization?
279. How do you feel about our organization?
280. How do you feel about this project?
281. What aspect of our program do you like the most? And why?
282. What is the best way to get your attention with the material we sent?
283. Why did you make your first gift to us?

284. You stopped giving to our organization. Why? How have we disappointed you?
285. When did you start giving money away and what made you begin?
286. What organization is the recipient of your largest gift? How much have you given them?
287. What would have to change to get us higher on your giving priority list?
288. What gift has given you the greatest joy?
289. How has the economy affected you?
290. Tell me what gift has caused the greatest disappointment.
291. What motivates you to give to the organizations you do?
292. What do you want most in life to achieve?
293. How would you like to be remembered?

About the Authors

Andrew Sobel and Jerry Panas have a relationship that is akin to that of Oscar and Felix in *The Odd Couple*. They continue to argue, however, about who is the obsessive Felix and who is most like the messy, laid-back Oscar.

In any event, they have followed surprisingly parallel paths in becoming the foremost authorities in their respective fields. Jerry is the world's leading authority on creating donors for life; Andrew, on how to develop clients for life. Through 70 combined years of experience advising and coaching leaders, they have learned to harness the power of great questions to deepen relationships, win new business, and influence others. *Power Questions* is the fruit of their unique collaboration.

Andrew Sobel

Andrew is the most widely published author in the world on client loyalty and the capabilities required to build trusted business relationships. His first book, the bestselling *Clients for Life*, defined an entire genre of business literature about client loyalty. His other books include *Making Rain* and the award-winning *All for One: Ten Strategies for Building Trusted Client Partnerships*.

For 30 years, Andrew has worked as both a consultant to senior management and an executive educator and coach. His clients have included leading corporations such as Citigroup, Xerox, and Cognizant, as well as professional service firms such as Ernst & Young, Booz Allen Hamilton, Towers Watson, and many others. His articles and work have been featured in a variety of publications such as the *New York Times, BusinessWeek*, and the *Harvard Business Review*. Andrew is a graduate of Middlebury College and earned his MBA at Dartmouth's Tuck School.

Andrew is an acclaimed keynote speaker who delivers idea-rich, high-energy speeches and seminars at major conferences and events. His topics include Developing Clients for Life; Creating a Rainmaking Organization; Collaborating to Grow Revenue; The Beatles Principles; and Win New Business and Build Relationships with Power Questions. He can be reached at http://andrewsobel .com.

Jerold Panas

Jerry is Executive Partner of Jerold Panas, Linzy & Partners, one of the world's most highly regarded firms in the field of fundraising services and financial resource development. His firm has served more than 2,500 client institutions since its founding in 1968. Jerry's clients comprise many of the foremost not-for-profit institutions in the world. They include every major university, museum, and health-care center in the United States. Internationally, Jerry has advised organizations as diverse as the University of Oxford, the American Hospital in Paris, and Nuestros Pequeños Hermanos in Mexico, the largest orphanage in the world.

Jerry is the author of 13 popular books, including the all-time bestsellers *Asking* and *Mega Gifts*. He is founder and chairman of the board of the Institute for Charitable Giving, one of the most significant providers of training in philanthropy.

Because of the prominence of the firm and the impact of Jerry's writing, few have had a greater influence in the history of the profession. He is a favorite speaker at conferences and workshops across the United States. He gives more than 50 keynote speeches a year with a variety of titles, including Shaking the Money Tree; Be the Best You Can Be; The Magic Partnership; Listen!; and I Hear a Gift, Aim High. He can be reached at http://jeroldpanas.com.